MODERN WORLD NATIONS

MODERN WORLD NATIONS

Venezuela

Richard A. Crooker
Kutztown University

Series Consulting Editor
Charles F. Gritzner
South Dakota State University

CHELSEA HOUSE PUBLISHERS
An imprint of Infobase Publishing

Frontispiece: Flag of Venezuela

Cover: A boy runs down a stairway in the Resplandor shantytown area of Caracas, Venezuela.

Venezuela

Copyright © 2006 by Infobase Publishing

All rights reserved. No part of this book may be reproduced or utilized in any form or by any means, electronic or mechanical, including photocopying, recording, or by any information storage or retrieval systems, without permission in writing from the publisher. For information contact:

Chelsea House
An imprint of Infobase Publishing
132 West 31st Street
New York NY 10001

Library of Congress Cataloging-in-Publication Data

Crooker, Richard A.
  Venezuela/Richard A. Crooker.
    p. cm.—(Modern world nations)
  Includes bibliographical references and index.
ISBN 0-7910-8834-0 (hard cover)
  1. Venezuela—Juvenile literature. I. Title. II. Series.
F2308.5.C76 2005
987—dc22   2005026621

Chelsea House books are available at special discounts when purchased in bulk quantities for businesses, associations, institutions, or sales promotions. Please call our Special Sales Department in New York at (212) 967-8800 or (800) 322-8755.

You can find Chelsea House on the World Wide Web at http://www.chelseahouse.com

Text and cover design by Takeshi Takahashi

Printed in the United States of America

Bang 21C 10 9 8 7 6 5 4 3 2

This book is printed on acid-free paper.

All links, web addresses, and Internet search terms were checked and verified to be correct at the time of publication. Because of the dynamic nature of the web, some addresses and links may have changed since publication and may no longer be valid.

Table of Contents

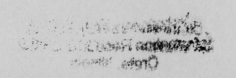

Venezuela

CHAPTER

1

Introduction

Venezuela sits prominently along the Atlantic and Caribbean coasts of northern South America. Colombia is to the west, Brazil to the south, and Guyana to the east. Venezuela's total area, which is medium-sized by South American standards, is roughly the combined size of Texas and Oklahoma. It is about one-tenth the size of Brazil (South America's largest country) but ten times larger than French Guiana (the continent's smallest country). Venezuela stretches from 1° to 12° north latitude. Close to the equator, it is a tropical country.

Tucked inside Venezuela's boundaries are some of the most diverse natural landscapes of South America. During a short drive south from the hot Caribbean shoreline to nearby mountain crests, the traveler sees a kaleidoscope of plants, from cacti to pine trees and from rain forests to alpine grasses. Traveling farther south and beyond the mountains, the unbounded plains of the country's midsection

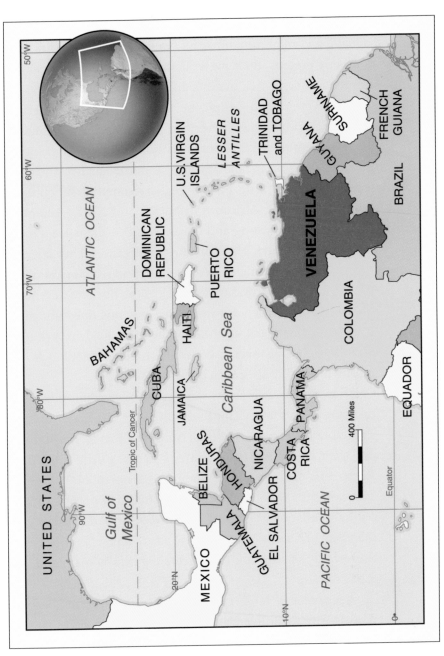

Venezuela is a tropical country that lies along the northern section of South America. It is bordered by Brazil on the south, Colombia on the west and southwest, and Guyana on the east. The Caribbean Sea forms the northern border. Venzuela is about the combined size of Texas and Oklahoma.

appear. Tall grasses, lazy streams, wily crocodiles, hungry jaguars, and migrating birds fill the land and sky. In the most southerly regions, the traveler discovers amazing tropical rain forests, a mineral-rich plateau, and magnificent waterfalls.

The Venezuelan people belong to the Latin American (Hispanic) culture. Nearly everyone speaks the Spanish language and is a member of the Roman Catholic Church. The culture, however, is by no means uniform. Venezuelans live and work together in a melting pot of vital overlapping subcultures: European, Indian, African, Caribbean, and North American. They are mostly young and urban. Most of them are a blend of races, a mixture of color and appearance. They identify themselves as Venezuelan because they share historical bonds to the land and cultural traditions like the fine arts and litera- ture. In general, they are easygoing, but this does not mean they are lazy or lack ambition. The vast majority are poor economically, but their warm smiles reflect a people who are fun-loving and confident in life.

Christopher Columbus was the first European to set eyes on Venezuela's shores. Alonzo de Ojeda (or Hojeda), a Spanish ship captain who came to South America a year after Columbus did, gets credit for the country's name. Ojeda landed on Aruba and Curaçao, two islands just north of Venezuela. There, natives were living in houses standing on poles in the sea like houses in Venice, Italy. In jest, one of Ojeda's crew members shouted "Venezuela!" ("little Venice"). Ojeda used the term in his logbook to describe the nearby mainland, and the name stuck.

Venezuela is most famous for beauty queens, baseball players, Simón Bolívar, and political instability. The annual Miss Venezuela Pageant is the most widely watched TV pro- gram. Baseball is the national spectator sport. Bolívar, South America's most famous nineteenth-century political figure, was born in Venezuela. He was the main hero in South America's fight for independence from Spain. He was a great leader who

With such a vast blending of races and cultures, Venezuela is rich with fine art and tradition. Here, two Venezuelans paint their faces with the national colors as a sign of national pride.

wanted to unify South America. Unfortunately, Bolívar died at a relatively young age. Otherwise, he could have perhaps stopped Venezuela's fall into 130 years of dictatorial rule and political conflict. Democracy finally replaced despotism in the mid-twentieth century, but the government has passed through several political crises since then.

As the twenty-first century unfolds, Venezuela is at a cross-road. A popular president seems serious about fighting the poverty that pervades the country. His political opponents and the United States, however, fear that he might be plotting to turn the country into another dictatorship or a Cuban-style communist state. Such a dramatic change could throw the country into violence and chaos. Venezuela's uncertain future is important to the United States and the world: It is the Western

Hemisphere's largest exporter of oil, much of which goes to the United States. We cannot predict what Venezuela will be like in the future. But a better understanding of Venezuela today will help us prepare for a better understanding of it tomorrow. Described here is how geography and history converged to create the nation of Venezuela as well as an outline of its future problems and prospects. We begin our study by exploring Venezuela's assorted physical landscapes, for the land is the stage on which a nation plays out its unique existence.

2

Physical Landscapes

The diversity of landforms, climate, plant life, soils, and wildlife has influenced Venezuela's history, economy, and settlement. All the same, a growing human population threatens the country's environment.

LANDFORMS

Venezuela has five major landform regions: Caribbean Margin, Northern Highlands, Orinoco Plains and Delta, Guiana Highlands, and Amazonas Plain. Each region's physical geography and natural resources have made important contributions to the development of Venezuela.

The Caribbean Margin

Squeezed between green mountains and the turquoise sea, this slender coastline is a small fraction of the country's total area. On

This is a view from above the city of La Guaira—a city on the Caribbean coastline. The Caribbean Margin is one of the five major landform regions of Venezuela.

the west end is the impressive, raindrop-shaped Maracaibo Lowland. A freshwater lake—Lake Maracaibo—fills much of the basin floor. A narrow strait connects the lake to the Gulf of Venezuela. Two ranges of the Andes Mountains define the lowland's rounded edges. The Sierra de Perijá range sits to the west, and the Sierra de Mérida range lies to the east and south. The rugged slopes of these mountains dip steeply toward Lake Maracaibo, enabling fast-flowing streams to wash deep layers of sediments into the lake and surrounding lowland.

The basin offers many landscape contrasts. The northern part is a sunburned, arid zone with thorny scrub. It has little or no farming. In the southern section, a green swampy rain forest, high humidity, and a near absence of wind make the air feel incredibly muggy. The southern zone's damp conditions support ferocious crocodiles, malaria-carrying mosquitoes, and blood-sucking ticks and leeches. During its early history, the whole basin was poor and neglected. Its few inhabitants eked out a living by subsistence agriculture and a little fishing. That all changed with the discovery of oil in 1917, a prelude to the opening up of one of the world's richest oilfields. Within a few years, oil derricks lined the lakeshore. Now, derricks even cover part of the lake itself and former lakeside villages are flourishing oil towns. The city of Maracaibo, which sits advantageously near the Caribbean's Gulf of Venezuela, is a main oil processing and shipping center and the country's second-largest city.

The Caribbean Margin has four peninsulas. At the western end, like the jaws of a nutcracker, the Guajira and Paraguaná peninsulas hem in the Gulf of Venezuela. Farther east, like obstinate siblings, the tips (capes) of the other two peninsulas point in opposite directions. The Araya Peninsula points west, runs parallel to the shore, and encloses the Gulf of Cariaco near Cumaná. The Paria Peninsula points east toward Trinidad Island. (Trinidad is part of the country of Trinidad and Tobago.) Early Spanish sailors named the narrow strait separating the Paria cape from Trinidad *Boca del Drago* (Dragon's Mouth). Together, the Peninsula of Paria and Trinidad Island outline the Gulf of Paria.

Venezuela's largest islands lie off the northeast coast, just north of the Araya Peninsula. Vitally important during early colonial times because of the pearl trade, these islands rapidly declined in significance with the collapse of the pearl fisheries and the growth of mainland settlements. The islands have regained their prominence in modern times. They are surrounded by the largest marine reserve in the Caribbean Sea. Additionally, the islands and the mainland coast are becoming important recreation and tourist centers because of their remarkable tropical beauty.

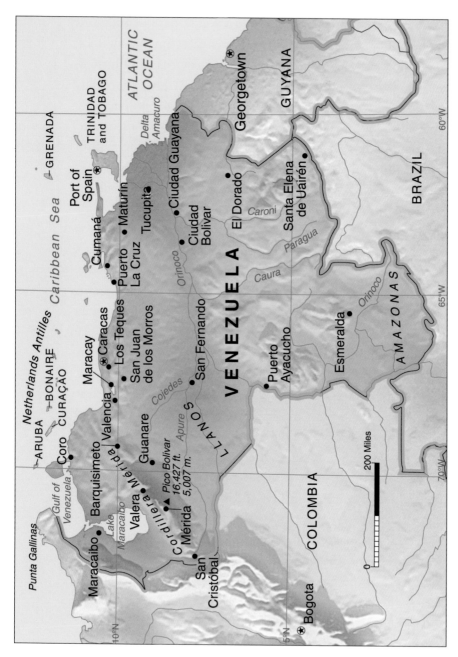

Venezuela's diverse topography has had a profound impact on the history, economy, and settlement of the country. The physical geography and natural resources of each area have influenced both the development of that region and of the country overall.

Northern Highlands

The Northern Highlands occupy almost one-third of the country. These mountains are, in fact, part of the crumbled edges of two tectonic plates (large sections of Earth's outer rock layer) that are slowly grinding past each other. The South American Plate is moving westward, and the Caribbean Plate is moving eastward. As the plates pass each other, the bump-and-slide motion gradually lifts the Earth's crust upward to form the highlands. In the distant past, volcanism accompanied the grinding plate movement, but no active volcanoes are found in Venezuela today. Unfortunately, however, violent earthquakes occur along faults (breaks) separating the plates. Venezuela's quakes are as powerful as those along the San Andreas Fault in California. Venezuela's most devastating earthquake took place in 1812, when Caracas was almost totally destroyed and 20,000 people died.

The Northern Highlands region has three subregions. At the western end is a branch of the Andes (Sierra de Mérida), the middle area is the Central Highlands, and the northeast end is the Northeast Highlands. Each subregion is different geologically. Elevations generally diminish from west to east. The Sierra de Mérida's summits exceed 15,000 feet (4,572 meters), whereas the Northeast Highlands barely reach half that height. The highest mountain in Venezuela is Pico Bolívar, which soars to 16,427 feet (5,007 meters) in the Sierra de Mérida. Alpine glaciers actually exist on Pico Bolívar and a few other lofty Sierra de Mérida peaks. These moving ice masses are slowly melting away. Ten glaciers existed in 1952, but only five remain today. Rising global temperatures are causing the wasting of glaciers in Andean South America and elsewhere in the world. Venezuela's last glacier will probably vanish within the next several decades.

Valleys of the Northern Highlands were magnets for Spanish settlement. Colonial towns thrived in the valleys, with their mild climates, reliable water supplies, and fertile alluvial soils. Today, this region is still home to the country's greatest population concentrations.

Orinoco Plains (Llanos) and Delta

This two-part (plains and delta) region occupies the middle of the country. The Orinoco River and its tributaries have transported thick layers of sediment from the Northern Highlands and the Colombian Andes to form the region. Venezuelans call the Orinoco Plains the *Llanos* (Spanish for "plains"). Natural grassland covers most of the Llanos, so this part of the region is important for grazing cattle. The plains are low-lying, however, and prone to river flooding, which hampers transportation and settlement. Sedimentary rocks lie beneath the plains. These porous rocks store valuable deposits of oil and natural gas, making the Llanos important to Venezuela's economy and future.

The second part of this region is the Orinoco River Delta, formed as the river empties into the Atlantic Ocean. Each year, the river carries 200,000 tons of silt and clay to the delta, which is still growing. In fact, the river deposits most of its muddy load on the ocean side of the delta, causing it to grow seaward at an impressive average annual rate of 144 feet (44 meters). The delta surface is a low-lying maze of plains and mangrove swamps. Its surface spans an arc of about 250 miles (400 kilometers) on the Atlantic Ocean side and tapers back into the river channel some 125 miles (200 kilometers).

The delta is not a pleasant area. Its climate is terribly hot and humid, it is infested with crocodiles and mosquitoes, and it has few resources. As a result, human occupation has been sparse, aside from a small indigenous Indian population.

Guiana Highlands

This region makes up the southernmost third of Venezuela, covering the state of Bolívar and part of Amazonas. The mountains extend short distances into neighboring Guyana and Brazil. Escarpments (steep slopes) separate the region from the lowlands of the Orinoco and Amazon rivers.

A striking landform feature of the Guiana Highlands is an elevated, grass-covered plain, the *Gran Sabana* (Spanish for "large treeless plain"). Other prominent features are *tepuis*, tabletop mesas that are unusual in their height and size. Tepuis (singular, *tepui*) are the remains of an ancient sandstone table-land overlying an even more ancient granitic rock.

The highest tabletop tepui is Mount Roraima (9,094 feet or 2,772 meters). This mountain marks the juncture of Venezuela, Guyana, and Brazil. The summit was the setting of Sir Arthur Conan Doyle's legendary 1912 book, *The Lost World*, which included terrifying dinosaurs and fiendish man-beasts roaming the mountain. Mount Roraima became Venezuela's most famous summit because of the book and the release of a popular Hollywood silent movie version in 1925.

Most streams flow northward from the Guiana Highlands to join the Orinoco River. The Caroní is the region's largest river, the major tributary of the Orinoco, and Venezuela's largest supplier of hydroelectric power. Several rivers descend rapidly over steep cliffs to produce spectacular waterfalls (*saltos* in Spanish). These roaring threads of falling water provide picturesque scenery for the tourist industry. A star attraction is Angel Falls. These waterfalls, the tallest in the world, make a dramatic 3,212-foot (979-meter) plunge off the edge of a large tepui.

Two thick granite ridges extend southwestward from the main part of the highlands—the Neblina and Parima ranges. The Neblina Mountains' highest peak reaches 9,886 feet (3,014 meters), making it the tallest mountain range on the continent east of the Andes. The Parima Mountains are where the Orinoco River begins its long journey to the Atlantic Ocean.

The Guiana Highlands' vast mineral deposits, including iron and gold-bearing ores, are important to Venezuela's

Mount Roraima stands tall in Canaima National Park, in southeastern Venezuela. The park is renowned for its *tepuis* (flat-topped mountains), and also inspired Sir Arthur Conan Doyle to write *The Lost World*.

economy. Indeed, the region would have no large settlements if it did not have valuable minerals. The area's rugged interior location tends to discourage road building, and its soils are generally sandy, acidic, and infertile for farming.

Amazonas Plain

This low-lying plain sweeps a wide band at the western edge of the Guiana Highlands. It lies wholly within the State of Amazonas, its namesake. Several dozen large tepuis, like those in the Guiana Highlands, rise above the plain. Plant life is variable, as savanna grasses blanket the region's northern half and tropical rain forest cover the southern half.

Three rivers dominate the plain. The Amazon River drains the southern third of the region by way of its largest tributary, the Negro River. The Orinoco River drains the remaining two thirds of the region. As a rule, rivers have their own drainage basins, as high ridges keep their tributaries separate from those of other streams. The Amazonas Plain, however, has no ridge to divide tributaries. As a result, a third river—the Casiquiere—flows across the plain as a tributary of both the Negro and the Orinoco rivers. This situation is highly unusual. Spanish missionaries first reported a Casiquiere "canal" connecting the drainage of the two rivers in the mid-1600s. Many Europeans, however, thought that such a river did not exist. In 1800, the famous German geographer Alexander von Humboldt and his French colleague Aimé Bonpland found and surveyed the celebrated river. Their journey to the Amazonas Plain is one of history's most interesting missions of scientific exploration, research, and discovery.

This region is an important refuge for some of Venezuela's most isolated indigenous tribes. Because of the plain's remoteness, the Indians have managed to retain important elements of their cultures. Little by little, however, cross-border incursions of miners and loggers from Brazil are threatening their land and way of life.

CLIMATES

Venezuela lies entirely in the tropics. Yet, its climate varies from desert to alpine. These huge variations result from topography (different elevations) and seasonal changes of the moist northeast trade winds. Differences in elevation cause most temperature variations in tropical climates. In fact, some of the world's highest yearly average temperatures occur in Venezuela's coastal lowlands and low-lying interior plains. The annual average temperature at Maracaibo, a coastal city, is 84°F (29°C). At Cumaná, another coastal city, it is 81°F (27°C), and at Ciudad Bolívar, a city in the interior Llanos, it is 83°F (28°C). In the mountains, temperatures are noticeably cooler. For example, the average temperature of Caracas, which is about 3,000 feet (914 meters) above sea level, is 74°F (23°C).

Von Humboldt was the first scientist to describe temperature changes in relation to different elevations in the Andean highlands of Venezuela, Colombia, and Ecuador. He identified three broad temperature zones: hot, temperate, and cold lands. The three zones vary slightly from region to region. In Venezuela, *tierra caliente* (hot land) begins in the lowlands and extends to an elevation of about 3,000 feet (914 meters). Temperatures range from 75° to 83°F (24° to 28°C). The *tierra templada* (temperate land) is roughly from 3,000 to 6,000 feet (914 to 1,829 meters), with readings from 65° to 77°F (18° to 25°C). *Tierra fria* (cold land), which is above 6,000 feet (1,829 meters), has much lower temperatures than the temperate zone. Up to roughly 10,000 feet (3,048 meters), temperatures range from 48° to 52°F (9° to 11°C). Above that elevation, average temperatures are below 46°F (8°C). Alpine conditions, including areas with snow cover and glaciers, begin around 10,000 feet (3,048 meters). Von Humboldt aptly noted that regardless of elevation, tropical temperatures tend to vary little from month to month, generally by only a few degrees. Geographers still use von Humboldt's concepts of temperature range and vertical zones of temperature to describe climates of all mountainous tropical regions, not just those in northern South America.

Temperature is not the only basis for classifying different climates in the tropics. Precipitation usually varies according to two seasons—summer and winter. Maximum rainfall occurs at the time of the highest sun (summer), while there is a distinct dry season at the time of the lowest sun (winter). In Venezuela, the summer or wet season extends from April to November and the winter or dry season through the rest of the year. Virtually all of Venezuela has a wet-dry tropical-type climate. Only along the north coast do changes to the type occur. For example, near-desert conditions prevail in Coro, a small town in the coastal northwest.

The source of moisture for Venezuela's summer rains is the northeast trade winds. Beginning in April and May, these winds churn the Caribbean Sea as they blow from the general direction of Puerto Rico toward South America's north coast. Arriving at the coast, they are full of moisture from the Caribbean's evaporating waters, but they pass over Venezuela's shore with not so much as a drizzle until the mountains lift them. The temperature of the rising air decreases quickly, forming giant, anvil-shaped thunderclouds. Resulting heavy afternoon downpours are typical. The northeast trades end in early November, as shifting global air pressure causes them to swing haltingly away from Venezuela. Cut off from the vaporous breath of the sea, the dry winter season sets in.

Venezuela's pattern of total annual rainfall ranges from parched to super wet. Rainfall in the coastal lowlands is so low that much of the area has a desert or semidesert climate. Coro has just 16 inches (406 millimeters) of precipitation, Maracaibo has 21 inches (533 millimeters), and Barcelona has 26 inches (660 millimeters). Most of the vast Llanos region gets a full 40 to 60 inches (1,016 to 1,524 millimeters). The coastal fringe of the Orinoco Delta gets 60 to 80 inches (1,524 to 2,032 millimeters). Parts of the Maracaibo Lowland and the Amazonas Plain catch more than 80 inches (2,032 millimeters).

PLANTS AND SOILS

Soil types vary in their ability to store water. This variation in soil moisture is part of the reason that natural plant groupings range from desert, where soils are thin and soil moisture is scarce, to tropical rain forest, where deep soils hold abundant moisture. A soil's blend of nutrients and minerals (plant food) is also a factor in plant growth.

The *tierra caliente* climate includes tropical rain forest. The forest's thick canopy of leaves and vines protects the soil from tropical heat and heavy rains. Unfortunately, Venezuelans have cleared away large areas of the lush forest and exposed the soil to water erosion and baking rays of the sun. As a result, Venezuelans no longer grow crops, harvest timber, and collect firewood in such areas.

Geographers call the forested area of this zone the "Zone of Tropical Products," as carefully managed crops of cassavas, sugar cane, bananas, and other water-demanding and warmth-loving plants can grow well there. Even so, forest clearing and erosion of soil are serious problems in the zone. There are still some sizable but shrinking areas of tropical rain forest in parts of the Maracaibo Basin, Orinoco Delta, Amazonas Plain, and Guiana Highlands. Certain slopes and valleys facing the northeast trade winds still have patches of this forest, even in the heavily populated areas of the Northern Highlands.

Savannas (tropical grasslands) grow in sub-humid parts of the *tierra caliente* zone, such as the Llanos. They are one of nature's responses to tropical climates that have an annual wet-dry rainfall pattern. The grasses are tall (at least waist high in many areas) and form a thick, protective layer over the soil. They survive a long, dry period for two main reasons. First, the grasses have shallow roots so that they can quickly absorb rainwater before it evaporates from the soil. Second, they

Venezuelan rain forests, such as this one in Machiques, Zulia, are known for large, lush trees and moist soil. Unfortunately, these areas are shrinking in size every day due to water erosion and forest clearing.

shade out competing plants. Savannas are natural pasturelands, but overgrazing can lead to soil erosion. As noted previously, the sweeping grasslands of the Llanos make up Venezuela's cattle-ranching heartland, but extensive areas are overgrazed. Drought-tolerant species of trees and palms are parts of the savanna landscape. They grow in groves along streams (gallery forests), or scattered and alone on the open plain.

Desert plants grow in the *tierra caliente* where rainfall is too low to support savanna grasses. Such plants are able to survive because they need only small amounts of nutrients and water. Desert grasses grow in widely spaced clumps. Certain small bushes are xerophytes (from Latin for "dry plants"). They have special adaptations to reduce moisture loss through leaves and stems. Other plants are succulents, like cacti and agaves. They have special "spongy" cells that store precious water. As in all dry lands, the amount of rainfall is meager so farming is difficult even in the most favorable places. Some of the country's poorest farmers eke out a living on the arid Guajira and Paraguaná peninsulas.

The *tierra templada* is pleasant for plants, as the moderate elevations of 3,000 to 6,000 feet (914 to 1,829 meters) compensate for the high temperatures of the low latitudes. A lush evergreen cloud forest grows in this zone. The forest has a closed canopy, colorful orchids, hanging vines, and delicate ferns. Alluvial (stream) deposits are a basis for fertile soils in the valleys. The agreeable climate and fertile valleys of the Northern Highlands are home to Venezuela's densest populations. Geographers refer to this region as the "Coffee Zone" in South America, because coffee is a typical commercial crop there.

Tierra fria, which begins about 6,000 feet (1,829 meters), is limited to high ridges and valleys in the Sierra de Mérida range and a few *tepuis* in the Guiana Highlands. A low, mossy elfin forest grows there, as infertile soils and cold temperatures stunt trees. Most slopes have thin soils. Erosion and landslides have removed much of the topsoil. This area is the "Zone of Grains," as farmers grow wheat and barley in warmer valleys wherever soils are fertile. Potatoes are an important root crop in the zone, where the upper limit of crop production is about 10,000 feet (3,048 meters).

Above that elevation, it is too cold and windy for trees or crops of any sort to survive. Geographers call this subzone the *páramo* (Spanish for "wasteland"). Cloud tops are often below the páramo because of the high elevation. As a result, precipitation is relatively low. Each afternoon, though, gentle breezes rising from the slopes below bring in a fine mist of water vapor that settles on the ground. Only hardy grasses and low-lying shrubs are able to live in the páramo's pebbly soil, rock crags, and cold climate. The economy there relies on the grazing of animals (cattle, sheep, and goats), as edible grasses survive to about 15,000 feet (4,572 meters) in elevation.

WILDLIFE

Venezuela's wide-ranging habitats result in highly diverse wildlife. The country has 284 species of amphibians, 341 of reptiles, 305 of mammals, 1,791 of fishes, and countless butterflies and other invertebrates. Moreover, the entire country is a birdwatcher's paradise. It is on a major seasonal migratory route of North American birds. Like clockwork, an armada of feathery travelers arrives from that continent to spend their winters in Venezuela or to stop on their way to destinations farther south. As a result, at least for part of the year, Venezuela is home to 1,360 species of birds, or roughly 15 percent of the world's known species.

The Caribbean shoreline and islands have many colorful birds and other animals, including egrets, flamingos, ibises, crab-eating raccoons, and green sea turtles. Besides migrating birds, the coastal mountains have sloths, monkeys, trogons, thrushes, and toucans as permanent residents. The elusive South American bear and Andean condor live in the Andean (Sierra de Merída) section. One of the world's most important bird reserves is the Llanos region. Birds flock there by the millions during the summer. Piranhas, electric eels, and crocodiles in the Orinoco River lie in wait for wading birds and other prey. The world's largest rodent, the web-footed capybara, is at home in water and on land. Gallery forests of the Llanos and mangrove swamps of the Orinoco Delta are home to caiman, anacondas (the world's largest snake), giant river otters, and howler monkeys. Giant anteaters, as well as armadillos, ocelots and jaguars, are in both areas.

Rain forests that cover large parts of the Guiana Highlands and the Amazonas are also rich in wildlife. The most remarkable variety of plant and animal life in these two regions resides

A scarlet macaw sits on a rain forest tree branch. Venezuela is among the top 15 countries in terms of biodiversity in the world and ranks seventh in the number of its bird species.

atop steep-walled tepuis. Each tepui has its own unique mix of rainforest plants and animals. Some species are even unique to a single tepui. Many of Venezuela's birds and other animals are on the endangered or the vulnerable species list, because humans are killing them or destroying their habitats.

THREATS TO NATURAL HABITATS AND WILDLIFE

A Swiss naturalist, Henri Pittier, was the first person to point out the ecological problems in Venezuela and the necessity to protect natural habitats. The first national park— the Henri Pittier National Park—was established in coastal mountains near Caracas in 1937. Now, there are 43 national parks. About three-fourths of the parks are in heavily populated northern Venezuela. The larger parks, several of which exceed the size of some U.S. states, are in more sparsely populated southern areas. For example, Parima-Tapirapecó National Park in Amazonas is twice the size of New Jersey.

Unfortunately, safeguarding against illegal settlement and exploitation is difficult, as the total area of parkland is enormous. Miners and land developers build illegal roads into protected areas. Ranchers and loggers cut timber along the roadsides to create open land for grazing livestock. Shifting cultivators move in. They burn trees for their nutrient-rich ash. New roads are also making it easier for game hunters to enter remote areas of the parks. Traders of live exotic animals (or skins, feathers, or body parts of dead animals) go to the parks as well to stalk and trap prey. In marine habitats, fishermen use motorboats to enter protected areas. Despite these significant setbacks, most people of Venezuela realize that plants and animals are important resources for the future and want to protect them. This realization is part of Venezuela's historical development, which is the subject of the next chapter.

3

Venezuela Through Time

And a river went out of Eden to water the garden;
and from thence it was parted, and became into four heads.
—HOLY BIBLE, GENESIS, CHAPTER 2, VERSE 10

COLUMBUS: GARDEN OF EDEN, CORN BEER, AND PEARLS

Christopher Columbus was the first known European explorer to see South America. He spotted the continent on the morning of July 31, 1498. Columbus was on his third voyage from Spain to the New World, when he saw a line of black mangroves with flocks of birds flying into the bright dawn. As the east-facing shore closed in, he saw the Orinoco River emptying its shimmering brown waters into the sea. He recalled that the Bible says the Garden of Eden, birthplace of the human race, lies in a land facing east with four great rivers flowing from it. The scene Columbus saw before him was so beautiful that he pondered whether the Orinoco might be one of the rivers of Eden. Columbus knew he had discovered a new continent from the size of the river (no mere island could produce a river so large). He began inspecting the landmass by sailing along its coastline toward the northwest.

The next morning, Columbus anchored off the southern shore of the Paria Peninsula. He came ashore after Indians there invited him and some of his crew to dine with them. Two things grabbed the Europeans' interest during their first contact: corn beer and pearls. The visitors were familiar with beer made from barley and hops, but the Indians made their beer, which they called *chicha*, from maize (corn). The Spaniards would eventually take some corn beer back to Spain, where it became popular for a brief time. More important, the guests noticed that their hosts were wearing necklaces with pearls as big as eyeballs. The natives told Columbus that the pearls, which the Europeans valued much more than beer, came from islands farther to the west.

Columbus sailed west from the peninsula of Paria until he came to an island where Indians dived for oyster-producing pearls. He traded trinkets for the pearls before he sailed north to Hispaniola (a Spanish colony of which he was governor). Although Columbus made a fourth voyage to the Caribbean, he never went back to Venezuela.

INDIANS AT CONTACT:
CARIBS, CHIBCHAS, AND CANNIBALISM

Venezuela's cultural landscape was a rich tapestry of colorful tribes when Columbus arrived there. Carib and Chibcha Indians accounted for the majority of the population. Several culturally distinct tribes that shared similar languages composed each of these groups. The Carib tribes lived along the Caribbean coast and adjoining Northern Highlands. (People of this group also inhabited many Caribbean Islands.) Chibcha tribes lived in the Andean section of the Northern Highlands. Their main center of culture was in the Andes of Colombia.

Indian villages included about 100 to 200 large houses with roofs shaped like tents. Roofs were made of stone in the mountains and made of bark, palm leaves, reeds, or straw in the lowlands. Inside the houses were hammocks for sleeping. The Indian diet was probably as good as or better than that of the Europeans. Crops included maize, sweet manioc, sweet potatoes, squash, chili peppers, pineapples, cacao, avocado, and guava. Women took care of the crops, made bread from bitter manioc (a root crop) and from corn, and raised ducks. They also spun cotton and made pottery. The men hunted and were excellent bowmen. Some rainforest dwellers dipped their arrows in curare, a deadly poison. Coastal Indians were expert canoeists. Fish and shellfish (clams, oysters, and mussels) from the sea were for the taking. Both lowlands and highlands had an abundance of game, including deer, tapirs, rabbits, pigeons, and quails.

Most tribes generally kept their enemies as slaves, permitted drunkenness during celebrations, smoked tobacco, used drums and flutes during dances, and divided the year into lunar months. The Indians of Venezuela, like Andean people from Colombia to northern Chile, chewed leaves of the coca bush. (The coca leaf is the modern world's source of the illicit drug cocaine.) Some tribes in Venezuela at times engaged in cannibalism, the eating of human flesh. They practiced this rare but heinous act on the bodies of fallen enemies as a ritual of conquest. For example, one tribe supposedly would cut off the arms and legs of any chief they captured and after he died, they would open his stomach and eat his intestines.

SPANISH CONQUEST:
PEARLS, SLAVES, GOLD, AND LAND (1500–1600)

[The conquerors] were hard men, cruel, rough, greedy for gold, and, yet, at the same time, as though inspired by a divine mission. They came from Spain in slow galleons plowing the sea, and at the first land they touched upon, they scattered like a flock of predatory birds.

—Arturo Uslar Pietri,
Las Lanzas Coloradas (*The Red Lances*, 1949)

Spain spent the sixteenth century taking control of its New World empire, including Venezuela. After Columbus reported his "discovery" of South America to the Spanish Crown, the Crown promptly sent expeditions to conquer the Indians and settle the lands there. The Crown dubbed members of such expeditions *conquistadors* (conquerors). Spain was in the midst of competing with other European powers for new territories that would yield valuable resources. The Crown agreed to let the *conquistadors* keep four-fifths of the money they earned from using the natural and human resources of the New World. The conquistadors found various resources in each region. Venezuela's major resources were pearls, slaves, gold, and fertile land.

Columbus's discovery of pearls in Venezuela was the most valuable result of his third voyage. The find also gave rise to the Indian slave trade in the colony. Indians used pearls as charms for adornment. They also traded them with interior tribes for corn, cacao (the source of chocolate), and other items. On the other hand, the Crown lusted for the white spheres, as they were rare in Europe and could bring in a hefty sum of money. Spaniards named the eastern shoreline of Venezuela where the pearls were traded the "Pearl Coast."

During the 1500s, the Pearl Coast was a major destination for pearl-hunting Spaniards who enslaved the native pearl divers. With strokes of the whip, the Spaniards forced the Indians to dive repeatedly, killing hundreds of them from exhaustion. To replace dead divers, the Spaniards carried out slave raids on the mainland. Later on, the slavers took the first Venezuelan Indians to work in the gold mines on Hispaniola.

The ruins of the former Spanish colonial city of New Cadiz are pictured here near the beach on Cubagua Island, an almost uninhabited scrub-covered islet off Venezuela's eastern coast. The Spaniards made Venezuela part of their sixteenth-century New World conquest.

Still later, they captured, branded, and sold Indian slaves to new sugar plantations on the Caribbean Islands.

By 1528, the Spanish Crown decided that Venezuela was not producing enough wealth to pay the cost of sending conquistadors there. As a result, the Crown gave control of the region to a group of German bankers led by the House of Welser. Under this deal, the Crown still sent Spanish conquistadors to the area, but they took orders from a German governor and German officers. The Crown owed the bankers money and hoped that the Germans could recoup the money by founding towns in the region. The Germans, however, were only interested in finding El Dorado, land of the Golden Man. According to legend, a Chibcha tribe in Colombia had an annual custom of smearing a chieftain with oil and rolling him in gold. He then washed off the gold in a sacred lake and also threw offerings of emeralds and gold into the waters. Europeans believed the story, which grew into a legend of a land of gold and plenty.

A series of explorers searched in vain for the celebrated El Dorado. The location of the mythical land shifted as conquerors explored new regions. German-led expeditions left from Coro and focused on the Maracaibo Basin, Venezuelan Andes, and western Llanos. The Germans sacked every Indian village they found, looking for gold and taking slaves. They never discovered riches in gold and never established any towns. Disgusted with the Germans, the Spanish Crown kicked them out of Venezuela in 1546. Within a decade, Spanish conquistadors found small gold deposits near the future sites of Barquisimeto and Caracas. They soon realized that Venezuela did not have large deposits of the precious metal. For the rest of the sixteenth century, the Spanish tried to hold onto their colony by fending off pirate attacks, developing agriculture, and establishing towns.

Pirates had been in the Caribbean Sea since the early 1500s. Spain was a nation almost perpetually at war with the English, French, or Dutch. These countries had small navies. Consequently, they hired pirates to do their dirty work in the Caribbean. The roll call of English pirates plying Venezuela's coast is the most infamous: John Hawkins (the reputed father of British piracy), Sir Francis Drake (the naval genius who helped destroy the Spanish Armada in 1588), Sir Walter Raleigh (the poet and ex-soldier), and Henry Morgan (the embittered ex-slave) all raided Venezuelan coastal towns. The invaders carried away much of the wealth that any townspeople had.

By 1600, despite costly raids by pirates, a sparse network of *haciendas* (large landholdings) spread along the mountains from Cumaná to Mérida. Hacienda owners were mainly former Spanish military officers to whom the Crown granted land for their loyal military service. Cattle and horses were raised on the haciendas. The owners also began to grow cacao for export about this time. Haciendas and cacao plantations depended on the *encomienda* system for laborers. An encomienda was a group of Indian villages. Villagers had to work for or pay a tribute to a specific Spanish landowner. The Indians also had to attend church regularly.

Landowners could employ Indians any way they wished—building, mining, or farming—but they did not own the Indians. Encomienda workers were supposed to be different from slaves. They could raise their own crops and livestock and live with their families in their own villages. Unfortunately, many Spaniards abused the Indians by making them work long, hard hours. Catholic missionaries pleaded on behalf of the Indians, but hacienda owners usually ignored their pleas. (Spain did not abolish the encomienda system until the mid-1700s.)

By 1600, a few small towns with Spanish and other European immigrants began sprouting up to serve the plantations and haciendas. Caracas, which had been the capital since 1577, enjoyed some prosperity. The seaports—Cumaná, Coro, Maracaibo, La Guaira, and Carabelleda—handled a small export trade in hides, cacao, flour, and cotton. Interior towns, like Tocuyo, Mérida, and Guanare, also became established. Roman Catholic priests were establishing missions to minister to Indians throughout Venezuela, even in remote places in the Llanos and in stream valleys of the Guiana Highlands.

ON THE SIDELINE:
FLOTAS, BASQUES, AND BEEF (1600–1800)

Despite Venezuela's strategic importance, the colony was slow to develop during the 1600s. The slow growth was mainly due to Venezuela's sparse supply of gold (the discovery of gold deposits in the Guiana Highlands would come later). The colony was also slow to grow because it was on the sidelines of the main Caribbean Sea routes. Spanish seaports in Cuba,

This is a view of the Caracas skyline. The nation's capital since 1577, Caracas is widely known for its contrast of impressive skyscrapers and rundown, less wealthy areas in the surrounding neighborhoods.

Hispaniola (today's Haiti and Dominican Republic), Puerto Rico, Colombia, Panama, and Mexico were flourishing. The success of these Spanish seaports centered on the transport of gold and silver from Mexico, Peru, and Bolivia to Spain. Huge *flotas* (treasure fleets) passing through the region stopped at these ports, but not at Venezuela's ports. Businesses at the other ports developed to serve the needs of crews, passengers, and growing populations. Even more prosperity came to the Caribbean islands in the 1700s from the expansion of plantation crops, especially sugar cane.

Venezuela was so poor that Spain was spending more money in governing the colony than it was collecting in taxes. Nevertheless, Spain needed Venezuela. Its location between the Caribbean Sea and the Portuguese colony of Brazil made it a buffer against Portuguese expansion into the Caribbean. What is more, the Dutch and English had island colonies nearby. Curaçao Island was an important Dutch colony, and the English held Trinidad. The Dutch and English were trying to set up colonies on mainland South America as well. Thus, the Spanish Crown decided to transfer control of its poor but strategically vital colony to an outside agency for a second time.

In 1728, economic control of the colony was given to the Caracas Company, a venture staffed and financed mainly by Basques from northeastern Spain. Basques had good business skills. The company ran Venezuela for more than 50 years, and the colony showed some signs of improvement. For example, in the mid-1700s, Europeans began their enduring love of chocolate, a by-product of cacao. The Caracas Company soon cornered the market for this product, and sun-drenched Venezuela became famous in Europe for its cacao.

Nevertheless, the Spanish colonists reacted negatively to the trade and tax policies of the Basques. The cacao planters around Caracas even staged unsuccessful revolts. Spain, fearing it could eventually lose the colony, dissolved the Caracas Company in 1789. The Crown then adopted a liberal policy of free trade between Venezuela and any country with which it was not at war. By 1800, the colony's economy was finally beginning to produce. Besides cacao, large farming estates (plantations) were exporting modest amounts of coffee, cotton, indigo, and molasses (from sugar cane) to Europe.

The colony's cattle industry in the Llanos was starting to impact the culture as well as the economy. The large ranches (haciendas) raised cattle primarily for their hides and leather, so there was plenty of leftover fresh meat. Beef became a staple of the Venezuelans' diet. Alexander von Humboldt, commenting in 1799, described "the consumption of meat being immense for this country." He noted that Caracas, with about one-tenth the population of Paris, "consumed more than half the beef annually used in the capital of France." More important, the cattle industry was boosting the colonial outpost's small export economy. Through the ports of Barcelona and Cumaná, the Llanos was becoming an important supplier of hides, leather goods (saddles, belts, hats, and chaps), tallow (for making soap), and salted beef to Spain and the Caribbean islands.

QUEST FOR INDEPENDENCE (1800–1830)

Three interrelated factors merged to give rise to the wars of independence in Spanish South America in the early nineteenth century. First was the ascent of an influential class of wealthy South American-born people of pure Spanish ancestry. They called themselves *criollos* or Creoles. The criollos ran thriving haciendas and plantations. They did not like that their economic position did not give them political power equal to that of Spanish *peninsulares* (Spaniards born in Spain). A second but related factor was economic. Landowners and merchants in the colonies had a growing sense of self-sufficiency and independence. Yet, they still had to pay high taxes on imported goods to Spain. The Spanish Crown spent most of its Venezuelan tax money (and that of its other colonies) to run its government in Madrid. Criollos and merchants wanted the Crown to invest more money in constructing public buildings, schools, and roads in the colonies.

A third factor that led to the wars of independence was the desire among many Spanish colonists to be free of outside control. The English American colonies' independence and the French Revolution's spirit of equality caused many Spanish colonists to question the right of Spain to control their affairs. The French Emperor Napoleon's takeover of the Spanish Crown in 1808 triggered the colonists' final break with Spain. Napoleon appointed his brother to run Spain. This event created a constitutional crisis in the Spanish colonies, as many colonists did not feel loyalty to a government no longer under Spanish rule. Venezuelan revolutionaries declared independence in 1811, but it would take a decade of bitter military conflict to fully secure self-government.

Simón Bolívar, *El Liberator* (The Liberator), was born in Caracas to a well-to-do criollo family. Ultimately, he would lead the revolution for independence that spread quickly throughout Spanish South America. Bolívar had military experience as a field commander in the Spanish Army. He was the most prominent of several revolutionaries who helped win the freedom of neighboring territories. The people of Venezuela, Colombia, Ecuador, Peru, and Bolivia still revere Bolívar for his part in gaining their independence. Bolívar and his generals won several key battles in Venezuela. His final drive to victory came from his stronghold at Angostura (today's Ciudad Bolívar) on the banks of the Orinoco River. His army included many Venezuelans, so they had a leading role in the overthrow of Spanish colonialism.

From 1821 to 1830, Venezuela existed as part of the Republic of Gran Colombia, a union also comprising current-day Colombia, Panama, and Ecuador. Bolívar served as president of Gran Colombia. The Republic was part of Bolívar's dream to unite all of Spanish America into a single country. Gran Colombia broke up, however, because regional interests were too strong. A separatist movement began in the Llanos region and quickly spread throughout Venezuela. Venezuela became a republic in its own right in 1830.

FROM CAUDILLOS TO DEMOCRACY (1830–PRESENT)

Venezuelans paid a high price for their independence. A lengthy war left their new country in ruins. People had no experience in self-government, because Spain had limited key colonial government jobs to European-born Spaniards. Besides, issues divided Venezuelans into regional factions from the beginning. People living in the Andes, Maracaibo Basin, Caracas Valley, Cumaná, and the Llanos had different economic needs and political aims. The new country needed experienced leaders who could unite the regions. Simón Bolívar felt that in time self-ruled countries could evolve in South America.

He was a proven leader and a Venezuelan. He might have stepped up as Venezuela's kindly dictator, but he died of tuberculosis in 1830, the year the colony became independent.

In the absence of strong leadership, a series of *caudillos* (military strongmen) rose to lead the regionally divided country. Caudillos were different from modern-day dictators in one important respect—they had absolute control over government. They made virtually all important government decisions. Caudillos ruled Venezuela from 1830 to 1935. After 1935, dictators began to share control with the legislature. General Marcos Pérez Jiménez was Venezuela's last (non-*caudillo*) dictator. He ruled from 1948 to 1958. The military overthrew Jiménez and handed over the country to moderate political leaders. In December 1958, the people elected Rómulo Betancourt president (he took office in February 1959), and presidents have been chosen by democratic elections ever since.

Democratic rule has not been easy. Right-wing military officers and left-wing guerrillas have threatened the country. Corruption and distrust in government still plague the country today. Political tensions are growing between the poverty-stricken lower class and the social elite. Dramatic fluctuations in oil prices have driven the country from one political crisis to another. Even so, Venezuelans are among the most diverse and best-educated people in South America. Perhaps they will eventually find needed solutions.

4

People and Culture

Beneath the beat of rock music, the incessant torrent of soap operas, and the innumerable movies made in Hollywood or Europe, the integrity of Venezuelan culture still remains intact in the Hispanic structure brought to America in the sixteenth century.
—JOHN V. LOMBARDI, VENEZUELA: THE SEARCH FOR ORDER, THE DREAM OF PROGRESS (1982)

Venezuela's population belongs to the Latin American (or Hispanic) culture, as almost everyone speaks Spanish and is Roman Catholic. The country's population of more than 25 million people is the fifth-largest in South America. Most people live in cities in the Caribbean Margin and the Northern Highlands, the regions that have had the longest history of European settlement.

POPULATION

The Caribbean Margin received the first Spanish settlements. Coastal Cumaná and Coro are two of the oldest European towns in South America, dating from the 1520s. Fertile highland valleys were settled next. The valleys were attractive for settlement because their climate is mild for their tropical location and because they have easy access to Caribbean trade routes. The last areas of European settlement were in the interior—the Llanos, Guiana Highlands, and Amazonas Plain—as a humid climate, seasonal floods, remoteness, and malaria made these areas less desirable to settle. In the twenty-first century, agriculture, commerce, oil, and tourism make the northern mountains the most populous part of the country.

A striking aspect of Venezuela is that 87 percent of its people live in *ciudads* (cities). Among South American countries, only Argentina has a higher percentage of city dwellers. Like two poles of a magnet, the cities of Maracaibo in Zulia State to the west and Petare in Miranda State to the east anchor a swath of heavy northern settlement. All three Venezuelan cities with a population of more than one million people are in the north.

Caracas, the nation's capital, is the largest city with a population of about 1.8 million. The floor of Caracas's valley is filled with glittering skyscrapers and teeming suburbs. Sprawling *barrios* (slum neighborhoods) festoon the western and eastern ends of the valley. Downtown streets are clogged with cars idling in traffic and sidewalk vendors hawking everything from fruit juice to leather goods. Boulevards shake to the rumble of subway trains rushing beneath them. The other two cities with more than one million residents are Maracaibo (1.6 million people) and Valencia (1.2 million people). The country has eight middle-sized cities, ranging in population from 300,000 to one million people. Five of these cities are in the urbanized north: Barquisimeto, Maracay, Petare, Barcelona, and Turmero. The other three, Maturín, Ciudad Guayana, and Ciudad Bolívar, are in the eastern Llanos.

Barrios surround every major city. They are a result of an ongoing migration of poor people from rural areas seeking jobs in cities. Poor Peruvians, Ecuadorians, Colombians, as well as Venezuelans, fuel this immigration. The barrios are overcrowded with people. As a result, they have inadequate schools, medical facilities, housing, streets, electricity, and sewer lines. Improving the living conditions of the barrios is a serious economic and political issue in Venezuela today.

Venezuela has a youthful population that is a strain on the economy. Forty-nine percent of the people are younger than 30 years old. Most people of this group are still in school, less skilled, or just starting their careers. Therefore, this group pays less in taxes for public services. Increasingly fewer people are in the middle (30 to 65 years old) and older age groups (65 years or older). The 30- to 65-year-old age group is the most productive. They tend to be highly skilled, earn more money, and therefore pay more taxes. Their taxes, in turn, make up most of the money that the government spends on schools, roads, health care, and fire and police protection. The problem is that the number of people in the middle group is too small to pay all the taxes for the public services that the other two age groups need.

Nowhere is the scarcity of tax revenues to meet the needs of population growth greater than in the barrios. In recent years, the government has channeled more oil revenues directly into barrios to improve public services there. Another hopeful sign is the decline of the annual population growth rate (births minus deaths). As a result, the population will gradually become less youthful in the future. Thus, the percentage of the total population in the higher-tax-paying middle-age group will gradually increase in coming decades.

RACE

Venezuela's population census does not include racial categories. Some people look definitely European, others purely

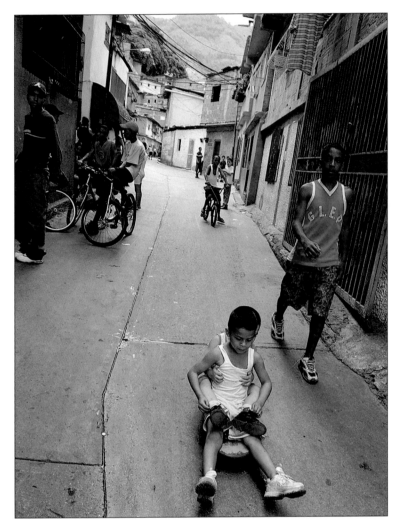

A Venezuelan child plays in the streets of Caracas. The youthful demographic makes up nearly half of the nation's population, but unfortunately is a strain on its economy.

Indian or African. A 1960s estimate said that Europeans (Spanish, Portuguese, Italians, and Germans) made up roughly 20 percent, blacks 8 percent, and Indians 2 percent of Venezuela's total population. About 70 percent was a blend of European, Indian, and African ancestry. Although no current estimate of racial categories exists, even a casual observer can see that the vast majority of Venezuelans belongs to the racially mixed group. There are people with copper skin, green eyes, and curly sandy hair. Others are light skinned with corkscrew hair and broad flattened noses. Still other people are dark-skinned with blue eyes, straight hair, and narrow bridged noses. The faces of the nation are truly random in their variety.

Since independence, races mixed to a large degree through marriage, and people grew to embrace their own racial identity as *Hecho en Venezuela* (Made in Venezuela). Today, Venezuelans are so racially mixed that they call themselves *criollos*, the term that American-born Spaniards used to identify themselves during colonial times. Venezuelans also use the racial terms *mestizo* and *mulatto*. A mestizo is a person of Indian and Spanish ancestry. A mulatto is a person of black and white descent. Social classes with rigid boundaries still exist. There is a poor, a middle, and a wealthy class. Color or appearance, however, is no longer the key barrier to social progress in Venezuela; economic opportunity is. Upward mobility of poor people is practically impossible, as they generally lack the basic skills to qualify for better-paying jobs. As we shall see in later chapters, this fact creates a dark cloud of social and political unrest.

CULTURAL VARIETY

Venezuelan society includes a variety of cultural as well as racial elements. During an errand-filled Saturday afternoon in Caracas, a female Ecuadorian household servant might run into a Venezuelan pharmacist, a Portuguese grocery store owner, and a Colombian taxi driver. At a shopping center, she might hear American rock music and see teenagers decked out in American-style clothes: designer jeans, tennis shoes, baseball caps, and T-shirts with slogans in English.

A tourist traveling from one part of the country to another would also witness various cultural scenes. Each region has its own flavor of music, food, dress, literature, and politics. The culture of a high-rise office worker of Caracas contrasts vividly with that of a Colombian immigrant working on an oil derrick in the Maracaibo Lowland. Similarly, the life of a cowboy in the Llanos differs from that of an Afro-Venezuelan cacao farmer living in a coastal valley. The culture of a Yanomami Indian of Amazonas is a world apart from all of these groups. This mixture of cultures and subcultures creates a varied, complex, and lively society.

Disappearing Indigenous Cultural Influence

Venezuela's Indian subcultures are rapidly disappearing, so they have little influence on society. No one knows for sure how many Indians lived in Venezuela before Columbus arrived. By the end of the first century of Spanish rule, European enslavement and disease killed off about 20 of the 50 or so original tribes. Most surviving Indians live in remote areas of the country where they have little contact with other Venezuelans.

The traditional way of living for Venezuela's surviving Indians cannot escape the spread of modern communication and transportation systems. These influences increase as the nation's overall population and demands for natural resources grow. The Venezuelan constitution provides for "the protection of indigenous communities and their progressive incorporation in the life of the nation." Even so, local political authorities seldom think of the interests of native people when making decisions affecting their lands, cultures, and traditions, or natural resources. Moreover, farmers and miners are intruding on their habitats, cutting down their forests, and polluting their water.

Surviving Indian groups live in the fringes of the Maracaibo Basin and in the Orinoco Delta, Guiana, and Amazonas areas. Altogether, 32 Indian tribal groups numbering about 300,000 people live in Venezuela. The main groups include the Guajira, north of Maracaibo; the Piaroa, Guajibo, Yekuana, and

Yanomami in the Amazonas; the Warao in the Orinoco Delta; and the Pemón in southeastern Guiana. These groups were originally hunters, gatherers, and shifting cultivators. They are currently adopting the language, religion, dress, crops, cultivation methods, and food habits of the dominant Hispanic culture at varying rates.

Afro-American Cultural Influence

Ancestors of Afro-Venezuelans began arriving in the early 1500s as slaves. Some came directly from Africa, others arrived from Colombia, but the majority came by way of the Caribbean islands. Venezuela abolished slavery in 1854. The descendents of black slaves still live in certain coastal valleys where their ancestors worked as servants and laborers on sugar-cane plantations. Few of them have retained their African and West Indian (Caribbean) identity. Another generation of blacks came to Venezuela in the twentieth century to work in the oilfields of Maracaibo and other areas. These migrants came from the Caribbean islands, particularly Trinidad. They still bear the imprint of Caribbean culture. In addition to Spanish, many speak English or French (depending on which island they came from).

The influence of African culture has survived mainly through African music. The heaviest concentrations of descendents of black slaves are in small towns and city neighborhoods, particularly in areas of eastern and southern Miranda State and in Aragua. The Afro-Venezuelan, hip-gyrating drums, rhythms and rituals of those areas reveal African roots. Afro-Caribbean musical imports, like salsa, meringue, rumba, reggae, and calypso beats, are widespread in northern cities and oil-rich parts of the Llanos.

European Cultural Influence

Spaniards certainly have had the greatest cultural impact among the great variety of people who migrated to Venezuela.

Piaroa Indian shaman Miguel Ochoa is pictured here with medicinal plants gathered from the jungle village of Aska aja, near Puerto Ayacucho. Venezuela is comprised of many different Indian tribal groups who are slowly adopting the nation's cultural ways.

During colonial times, most of them came from the Andalusia region in southern Spain. They formed a privileged class and made the rules by which everyone else had to live. Spanish colonial society centered on Spanish language, law, and religion. Spaniards preferred using slaves, servants, and wage laborers to do basic hand labor. During colonial times, Venezuela failed to attract poorer Spanish settlers, as the white elite had taken most of the good land. Moreover, a pitiful road system discouraged settlers from moving into poorer land on the margins of settled areas.

Not all whites belonged to the social upper class. Immigrants from the Canary Islands, which was a Spanish colony, and Basques from Spain became hardworking artisans and merchants. Venezuela continued to offer few chances for economic gain after independence. Unlike leaders of other countries in the Western Hemisphere, Venezuela's caudillo presidents had little interest in bringing in migrants to settle new land. An exception was a small group of German Catholics who relocated to the country in 1843. They founded Tovar, a colony near Caracas, and became successful cacao growers.

European influence became more diverse during the twentieth century. A large number of Spaniards came to Venezuela and other South American countries during the 1930s. The Spanish Civil War took place then, resulting in the rise to power of a fascist government (a hate-filled racist political dictatorship). From the 1930s through the 1950s, many Spaniards with anti-fascist political views fled Spain. Generally, they had college degrees. They quickly found places of influence in medicine, politics, government, education, literature and art in their adopted country. A more diverse group of Europeans came after World War II. This group included skilled workers from Spain, Italy, and Portugal. They ended up in and around Caracas. Members of this group became owners of various construction and retail businesses.

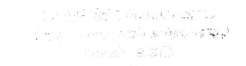

European immigration slowed to a trickle when a fiscal slump hit the country in the 1970s and has remained slow ever since.

U.S. Cultural Influence

U.S. cultural influence began with the start of Venezuelan oil production in the 1920s and 1930s. As time went along, oil money boosted the economy and created a wealthy class of businessmen who made shopping trips to the United States. Many well-to-do families began sending their children to schools there. These early contacts led to a growing taste for American consumer goods. The "Americanization" of Venezuelan culture accelerated in the 1960s and 1970s as "petrodollars" (petroleum dollars) spread to a growing middle class. The current Venezuelan obsessions with beauty contests, baseball, cars, fast-food restaurants, and TV are all U.S. hallmarks. American TV programs, in particular, have spread the American influence to all classes of Venezuelan society. Nevertheless, American culture does not dominate the country by any means. It is just a light tint on the artist's cultural palette; the brightest splashes of color on the cultural landscape are still intensely Venezuelan.

The Venezuelan Melting Pot

Venezuela is an example of a large melting pot—a place where people of diverse backgrounds mingle racially and culturally. Nearly all Venezuelans are criollos, or products of unions between the country's indigenous peoples, Africans, and Europeans. The sharing of cultural traits as well as racial mixing was inevitable. The physical appearance of the people attests to racial mixing. Cultural sharing is equally apparent. For example, most Indian tribes are adopting or already using Spanish as a second language. Conversely, Spaniards have used indigenous words in naming many towns, mountains, and rivers. Afro-Venezuelans' influence on music is obvious. So is cassava, a nutritious African root crop that is a staple in the

Venezuelan diet. The American influence, as we have seen, shows up in various superficial ways.

RELIGION

Ninety-six percent of the population claims membership in the Roman Catholic Church, but only about 20 percent attend services regularly. Almost all other Venezuelans belong to Protestant churches or sects. As in other Latin American countries, being Catholic does not stop Venezuelans from adding other rituals and spirits from indigenous and African religions. Students of religion call this form of Catholicism "Popular Catholicism." Popular Catholicism varies according to the traditions of priests from locale to locale, as no written doctrine guides its practice. The church accepts these traditions, as long as the priests who follow them stick to certain basic teachings of the Roman Catholic religion.

Two Venezuelan cult figures have a large number of devotees and receive respect from the church. The first is Madre María de San José (1875–1967). She died in a convent at Maracay where she spent most of her life. She worked in schools and hospitals there. Church members attributed many miracles to her care of the poor and the sick during her lifetime. Pope John Paul II confirmed her beatification (miracle work and spiritual purity) in 1995. She became the first Venezuelan to attain such status. Eventually, she could attain sainthood, the highest honor the Roman Catholic Church bestows to a devotee.

The second cult figure to receive the church's respect is the physician José Gregorio Hernández (1864–1919). He was born in a small town in the Venezuelan Andes. Like María de San José, he was a devout Catholic who cared for the poor and the sick. He became known as "the Doctor of the Poor," as he bought medicine for his poorest patients. His life ended abruptly, when a car struck and killed him in a Caracas street. His fame grew rapidly after his death. Hernández is more

Naiguata devils fall to their knees during the Corpus Christi festivities in Venezuela. This is considered one of the most spectacular folk celebrations that combines Catholic and pagan costumes.

revered than Madre María. Figurines and images depict a humble mustachioed man in a black suit, hat, and tie, holding a medical bag. They are found all over Venezuela, Colombia, and Ecuador. His image even appears on bottles of medicine. A campaign to declare him a saint has significant support.

VENEZUELAN IDENTITY

A nation-state is a group of people with a territory, an economic life, a distinctive culture, and a language in common. People identify themselves as "belonging" to a nation for complex reasons. Certainly, politics and government remind them daily of their nationhood. However, a people's pride in and enjoyment of their country's musicians, artists, writers, and poets are also important in their sense of national identity. The arts include the fine arts (music, dance, theater, and cinema), visual arts (painting, sculpture, and photography), and folk or traditional arts (handicrafts).

Venezuelans of different regions and subcultures share a love for certain kinds of music. Wherever you go—market, theater, or restaurant—you are surrounded by lively rhythms of salsa driven by African drumbeats. *Un Solo Pueblo* (One Single People) is perhaps the best-known traditional band. Their appeal is countrywide because they play a variety of Venezuela's folk music. To capture authentic sounds, they use the ukulele-like *cuatro* (a traditional four-stringed instrument) of the Llanos and the *tambor* or drum of Barlovento and other coastal areas. Their music also includes improvised lyrics of *llaneros* (Venezuelan cowboys); exuberant dances of Afro-Venezuelans; tender, wistful waltzes of Andeans; and English calypsos of Caribbean blacks.

Dance is also a vital part of being Venezuelan. This fact is not surprising given the importance of music. A popular guidebook on Venezuela noted, "Dancing here is more than a pastime—it is an essential social skill." Venezuela also has a strong theater tradition. Caracas is the nation's theater center, but groups perform in all major cities. Venezuelans also take pride in having a strong tradition in the visual arts. Public buildings and plazas throughout the country display the works of Venezuelan painters, sculptors, and architects.

Venezuela's rich body of literature has helped develop a strong Venezuelan identity. Rómulo Gallegos (1884–1969) and Arturo Uslar Pietri (1906–2001) are Venezuela's most important writers in this regard, because their writings remind Venezuelans about their common history. *Doña Barbara* is Gallegos's most influential novel. It pits Doña Barbara, a cruel woman who owns a large hacienda in the Llanos region, against Santos Luzardo, a small landowner who tries to keep her from taking his land. Although fictional, *Doña Barbara* uses local political innuendo to portray the corruption and brutality of Venezuela's reigning caudillo government.

Luzardo, the underdog, prevails against tyranny and emerges as a heroic llanero figure. The book's powerful imagery describes the llanero's mixed racial heritage and the bond between him and the land. Largely through *Doña Barbara,* Venezuelans see in the bygone llanero a symbol of their racial and cultural legacy (even though most of them are northern city folk who have never sat on a horse, seen a live cow, or set foot in the Llanos). Gallegos was elected president of Venezuela in 1948 largely because of the popularity of his novels. Unfortunately, he was not an adept politician and was ousted in a military coup only nine months into his term.

Arturo Uslar Pietri wrote short stories as well as novels. His most famous novel—*Las Lanzas Coloradas* (*The Red Lances*)—is a vivid description of Venezuela's wars of independence and its landscapes. Although published in 1931, it remains very popular and contributes to the Venezuelan sense of nationalism. Uslar also wrote poetry, short stories, and plays, and received several nominations for the Nobel Prize for literature. Like Gallegos, Uslar branched out from writing. He served as a government minister, journalist, senator, and even had a brief stint as a television pundit. Translations of *Doña Barbara* and *Las Lanzas Coloradas* are available in English. Gallegos's and Uslar's writings spanned most of the last century. Through their influence, Venezuelans have a better sense of their identity as a unique Hispanic nation as the twenty-first century is unfolding.

CHAPTER

5

Government and Politics

Government is not reason, it is not eloquence, it is force;
like fire, a troublesome servant and a fearful master.
Never for a moment should it be left to irresponsible action.
—GEORGE WASHINGTON,
U.S. PRESIDENT 1789–1797

Venezuela has rarely had a stable government. After independence—to use George Washington's words—Venezuela's government was "a troublesome servant and a fearful master," as the new nation was ruled by a series of irresponsible, self-serving dictators. The dictators rose to power through coups and rigged elections. Each dictator had an idea of what government should be like. As a result, the country had nearly 30 constitutions during its first 130 years of existence. Venezuela adopted a democratic form of government in 1959. The government has had several crises since then, but it has managed to have an unbroken succession of constitutionally elected presidents.

POLITICAL STATES

Venezuela's modern states sprang from three Spanish colonial departments: Caracas-Barinas, Zulia, and Orinoco. Spain ran the departments as economic zones: central, eastern periphery, and western periphery. Each zone was relatively independent and had three subareas: coastal, mountain, and Llanos. The coastal section had at least one Caribbean seaport. Mountain valleys supplied cacao, cotton, indigo, tobacco, and coffee to the seaports. The cattle-raising Llanos supplied cowhides for leather goods, tallow for soap, and dried beef. A primitive network of ox-cart trails tied the three subareas of each economic region together. The early economic regions competed with one another for the same export markets. This competition bred political disputes among the regions after Venezuela became self-governing.

Venezuela began dividing the former colonial departments into states as its growing population spread into previously unsettled areas. Today, Venezuela has 23 states and one federal district. Caracas became the capital and the nation's federal district as it developed strong economic and political ties to the rest of the country.

CONSTITUTION

The Constitution of 1999 defines the political system today. Changes to the constitution since then have given more power to the president. The document names Venezuela the "Bolívarian Republic of Venezuela," after the South American independence hero Simón Bolívar. It grants the right to vote to anyone who is age 18 or older, and it designates five branches of government. The president or chief executive leads the executive branch. People elect the president by a plurality vote (the candidate receiving the greatest number of votes). Presidents serve a term of six years and may be reelected to a single consecutive term. The president appoints a vice president, decides the size and composition of the cabinet, and makes appointments to it with input from the National Assembly.

The National Assembly, the second branch of government, is unicameral, meaning it consists of one voting body—the Chamber of Deputies. Voters in state municipalities and the federal district elect the deputies. (Venezuela's state municipalities are similar to U.S. counties.) The number of deputies for each municipality and the federal district is relative to the size of their populations. Indigenous people also are represented by three deputies. Deputies of the National Assembly serve five-year terms and may be reelected for a maximum of two additional terms.

The third division of government is the judicial branch. The Supreme Tribunal of Justice, which consists of 32 justices, heads this division. Justices are appointed by the National Assembly. Justices decide the legality of cases that have traveled through lower courts on appeal. They serve one 12-year term. The lower courts include district courts, municipal courts, and local civil courts

A citizens' branch forms the fourth part of the government. It consists of three people who are appointed to seven-year terms by the National Assembly. Among other things, this body can question the legality and constitutionality of decisions made by the Supreme Tribunal of Justice. The fifth branch of government is the five-member National Electoral Council (NEC). Members are elected by the National Assembly to seven-year terms. The NEC organizes elections at national, state, and local levels. A public petition signed by no less than 0.1 percent of registered voters can also start legislation or force the president to hold unscheduled elections. The NEC determines whether voters' signatures on the referendum are valid. This body cannot propose law-making bills and other legislation, but the other four branches may.

The unicameral Venezuelan National Assembly (VNA) votes on an item of legislation. Located in Caracas, the VNA is one of the nation's five different branches of government.

POLITICAL PARTIES

Political parties that represent the interests of citizens became possible in 1935, when General Juan Vincent Gómez's dictatorship (1908–1935) ended with his death. During his rule, the Venezuelan oil industry was changing the nation from a backward land of cattle-raising estates to a progressive country with a growing middle class. That middle class, however, needed more say in government to make the new economy work efficiently.

Transition to Democracy (1935–1958)

Dictatorships after Gómez allowed the legislature to have more power in decision-making. Thus, Venezuelan political leaders, many of whom had been imprisoned by Gómez or were living in exile, gradually worked their way back into political life. They moved the country toward democracy by organizing political parties. Three parties formed in the 1940s: Democratic Action (AD), Christian Democratic Party (COPEI), and Democratic Republican Union (URD). These parties participated in the selection of Venezuela's first democratically elected president, Rómulo Gallegos, the famous writer. His presidency lasted only nine months before a military coup threw him out of office in 1948.

In the mid-1950s, Marcos Pérez Jiménez, the country's last (non-caudillo) dictator, outlawed the parties because he felt they were gaining too much influence in decision-making. The parties returned, though, when the Venezuelan military forced Jiménez to flee to the United States in 1958. After a successful coup, Venezuela's military leaders would usually organize around a new dictator, but this time they broke the vicious cycle of dictatorships. A long history of waste and greed by dictators turned the coup leaders off to the idea of naming another dictator. In a dramatic move, the military leaders shifted power to civilian control. The AD, COPEI, and URD parties became legal again. In 1958, party leaders signed the Pact of Punto Fijo. (*Punto Fijo* is the name of a residence of a former Venezuelan president where the parties made the pact.) The three parties agreed to share power by appointing members from each body to presidential cabinets and government ministries.

Democracy (1959–2005)

The Punto Fijo deal made it difficult for parties other than the AD, COPEI, and URD to gain power in national politics. Therefore, Venezuelan democracy had limits. All the same, the main political parties had a greater role in government. This partial or so-called Punto Fijo democracy lasted from 1959 to 1998. The AD and COPEI became the dominant parties during the period. Both parties, however, failed to pay enough attention to the growth of poverty and the rise of political discontent in the lower class. As a result, in the 1990s, the two-party system unraveled and was replaced by a multiparty system.

The charismatic Hugo Chávez organized the largest new party—the Movement of the Fifth Republic (MVR)—in 1998. Chávez was a former military officer who led an unsuccessful military coup in 1992. Running as a left-wing populist, he led the MVR to victory in the December 1998 elections. He claimed Simón Bolívar's life and ideas inspired him to seek the presidency. Chávez also promised broad reform, constitutional change, and a crackdown on corruption. He won in a landslide because he had the support of the impoverished majority. The MVR has enjoyed a huge plurality of seats in the National Assembly ever since. Chávez oversaw the creation of a new constitution in 1999, which called for a new election in 2000. He easily won that election with 59.7 percent of the vote.

THREE CRISES OF VENEZUELAN DEMOCRACY

Venezuela has had an uninterrupted but shaky democracy ever since the military cast out General Marcos Pérez Jiménez in 1958. The people elected Rómulo Betancourt president, and he carried out his full term (1959–1964). His election began a succession of democratically elected presidents to the present. Even so, three political crises have threatened Venezuelan democracy since 1959.

Democracy was first tested during the 1960s by a guerrilla war. The rebels called themselves the *Fuerzas Armadas de Liberacíon Nacional,* or FALN (Armed Forces of National Liberation). FALN was a coalition of several political groups, the largest being the Communist Party of Venezuela (PCV). The FALN revolt was in the Andean states of Falcón, Mérida, and Táchira. Fidel Castro, the communist dictator of Cuba, gave arms and training to the rebels. Many FALN operations grabbed headlines in world news reports. The group kidnapped prominent people (including a famous Venezuelan soccer player), seized an ocean freighter, and hijacked an airplane in mid-flight (the first political air hijacking in history). The guerrillas tried to set up "liberated zones" in the countryside, as Castro had done when he took over Cuba. Their success depended on attracting recruits among the rural poor. FALN assumed incorrectly that peasants would join the revolt since they owned no land and received shamefully low wages from wealthy property owners.

FALN was surprised that its revolt did not win popular support in rural areas. The revolt did not receive support for two reasons. First, many peasants had moved to the cities in search of jobs. Second, the peasants who remained in the countryside believed that the government was going to make good on its promise to redistribute land from large haciendas to them. In 1967, the Communist Party withdrew from FALN and ended its role in the hostilities. In 1969, Venezuela legalized the party, so that its members could join in elections. A much smaller FALN rebel group fought in the state of Falcón into the 1970s.

A second crisis threatened Venezuela's democracy in 1989–1992. After a long period of declining oil prices, as well as government waste and corruption, the country's treasury was nearly empty. The government owed a huge foreign debt. Food prices were rising, and public services were declining. To stem the fiscal bleeding, newly elected president Carlos Andrés Pérez launched a strict economic program. He raised taxes, increased prices on public transportation, and reduced spending on social reforms. These measures were probably necessary to return Venezuela's economy to a sound footing. However, they meant additional hardships for the majority of people who were poor already. The specter of added poverty was too much for them. They rioted in major cities across the country. Pérez restored order by calling in the military, but only after soldiers' bullets killed more than 200 protesters.

Pérez's policies soon alienated officers of the military. He wanted to cut their salaries to help reduce the national debt. In

February 1992, a group of army officers led by Hugo Chávez mounted an unsuccessful coup attempt. A second failed attempt by other officers followed in November 1992. A year later, the Venezuelan Supreme Court forced Pérez to leave office for allegedly stealing or misusing millions of dollars in public funds. He was legally replaced with an interim president. This chain of events did not end Venezuela's record of freely elected governments, as the Supreme Court used constitutional means to remove Pérez from office.

A third crisis faced by Venezuela's democracy came in 2001–2004, during Hugo Chávez's first term as president. His policies met with increasing hostility from the middle and upper classes. Opponents feared another dictatorship was looming, and they made a strong case. Chávez got the legislature to pass a law allowing him to rule by decree during 2001. That year, he passed 49 laws by decree. In effect, these decrees let him run the economy, control the news media, and increase the political role of the armed forces. Chávez also appointed friends and allies to top state and business positions. There was also a mounting belief that Chávez was not delivering on his election promises to reduce poverty.

The growing dissatisfaction over Chávez led to national worker strikes and street riots. Political opponents got enough voters to sign a referendum that called for an election in 2004 to recall Chávez. Many political experts predicted Chávez would lose the election. His power base, the poor people of shantytowns across the nation, however, did not fail him. Record numbers of voters turned out. Election officials had to extend voting hours because the lines were so long. Chávez won 59 percent of the vote. Independent observers, including those from the prestigious Carter Center (founded by former U.S. President Jimmy Carter), declared that the election results were valid. Chávez's popularity was probably never greater than after his opponents' failed effort to remove him from

Venezuelan president Hugo Chavez meets with supporters in Caracas. His empathy with the poor neighborhoods of the nation won him the most recent election in 2004.

office. A few weeks later, Venezuela held elections for state governors. Pro-Chávez candidates won 20 of 22 available governor positions.

GOVERNMENT CORRUPTION

Corruption involving governmental officials (such as legislators, judges, prosecutors, mayors, and police officers) usually involves criminal acts of bribery, extortion, fraud, or money-laundering. Government corruption takes place to some degree in every country, but in Venezuela, it is a way of life. The U.S. State Department and human-rights organizations allege that government corruption is most widespread among judges and lawyers in the court system. The corruption is purportedly from a number of sources, ranging from drug kingpins to the executive branch of government.

Corruption, in one way or another, affects a nation's economy by driving up prices or by lowering wages. For instance, a government official may ask for a bribe of thousands of dollars before awarding a multimillion-dollar government contract to a private company. The company that pays the bribe then raises prices or cuts wages in order to pay the bribe. Although difficult to prove, "greasing the palm" of government officials with bribes is a common practice in the Venezuelan business world.

Extortion is taking money from someone by threatening or by harming the person or the person's friends or relatives. Threats often involve misused authority. For instance, Venezuelan police and state security forces allegedly extort money from citizens by threatening them with unlawful arrest or by refusing them protection from gangs unless they pay a "protection fee."

Fraud, a third form of corruption, usually involves hiding the truth in order to make money. It is so common among public servants in Venezuela that visitors to a government office may not even know that the person at the counter is lying to them. Kitt Baguley, the author of *Culture Shock! Venezuela*, described the frustration of setting up a business in the country: "Someone might tell you that there is a certain fee for a particular service, and for all you know there is. The only truth you can be certain of is that if you pay the 'charge,' your business will move ahead much more speedily."

Venezuela is a renowned money-laundering country. The goal of money-laundering is to hide the origin of illegal money. Criminals have money to hide. Bank employees make the money appear "clean" or legal by putting it in accounts of phony businesses. Employees receive a payoff for their part in the laundering scheme. In Venezuela, laundering huge amounts of money from selling drugs or from taking bribes for oil contracts is a common practice. Laundering drug money keeps drug kingpins and street pushers in business. It also contributes to the cycle of poverty and despair in barrios. Hiding bribe money from oil deals raises the cost of government programs that rely on petrodollars (oil money) to build highways, expand irrigation, and feed, shelter, and educate the poor. The removal of President Carlos Andrés Pérez in 1993 was due in part to his administration's involvement in an alleged money-laundering scheme.

FOREIGN RELATIONS

Venezuela is active in the international community. It is a founding member of the United Nations, the main world body of international diplomacy. The country has served several two-year terms on the United Nations Security Council and has been a member of the United Nations Commission on Human Rights. Venezuela is active in several key Latin American diplomatic organizations: the Rio Group (an organization of 19 Latin American and Caribbean countries); the Andean Community (Bolivia, Colombia, Ecuador, and Peru are the other members); and the Association of Caribbean States. Moreover, Venezuela is a member of the Organization of American States (OAS), which also includes the United States and 32 other countries in the Western Hemisphere.

Venezuela has border disputes with all its neighbors. Relations with Guyana are difficult, as Venezuela's claim would shift the boundary eastward to the Essequibo River, thus taking roughly three-quarters of Guyana's territory. Venezuela has periodically renewed its claim to the disputed territory. Venezuela has problems along its border with Brazil as well. Brazilian logging companies are sneaking into remote areas in Amazonas and the Guiana Highlands and plundering rain forests there. Moreover, squatters from Brazil are moving into the logged areas to farm the land.

The disputes with Colombia are more diverse. Venezuela's north coast location makes it a major transit country for cocaine and heroin shipments from South America to North

A main player in the international scene, Venezuela is active in multiple organizations, such as the Organization of American States. Here, members of the board speak on territorial problems within their country.

America. The country's Andean neighbors (Colombia, Peru, and Bolivia) produce the drugs. The drugs are brought to Venezuela overland and by airplane, usually from Colombia. As we have noted, the laundering of drug money and its use to bribe Venezuelan judges are major concerns. The United States is working with the country to combat drug trafficking. Another border problem is the large number of illegal Colombian immigrants entering Venezuela. Colombian rebel groups also cross the border to escape detection by the Colombian Army. The two countries also dispute the maritime boundary in the Gulf of Venezuela. The offshore area has valuable fish and petroleum resources. Venezuela and Colombia have established bilateral commissions to discuss these issues.

Venezuela's political relations with the United States are important, as the United States is its main trading partner. During the Punto Fijo years (1959–1998), few Venezuelan policymakers questioned U.S. foreign policies. President Hugo Chávez's government, however, has strained relations. Chávez's combative style of diplomacy toward the United States is reminiscent of a caudillo bully. For instance, in his speeches he has called the United States a terrorist country and the U.S. president obscene names. More serious, Chávez is a vocal opponent of the 2003 U.S. invasion of Iraq. He also defended Iran's nuclear program in 2005, even though the United States feared that Iran could use the program to develop nuclear weapons.

The greatest damage that Chávez has done to Venezuela-U.S. relations is through his friendship with Cuba's leader, Fidel Castro. Castro is an enemy of the United States. He is the only dictator in Latin America, and he leads the only communist regime in the Western Hemisphere. The United States worries that Chávez is turning into another Castro. He has opened up trade relations with Cuba and has pursued a series of Cuba-style political initiatives. One such initiative is taking over foreign-owned land in Venezuela and creating "Bolivarian Circles," groups of civilians similar to Castro's government-run cooperatives.

There are trade agreements between Venezuela and the United States, despite Chávez's unfriendly policies. The United States desperately needs Venezuela's oil. On the other hand, Venezuela needs the United States, as the United States provides about 30 percent of Venezuela's imports and purchases roughly 50 percent of its exports. In the near term, trade and diplomacy between the two countries are likely to continue, because the countries' economies need each other.

6

Economy

*The first European explorers had noticed a strange
black material [oil] in the lake and swampy shores
of Maracaibo. The indigenous communities used
the sticky fluid to caulk and repair their canoes and
to trap animals. The Spaniards dismissed
the "devil's excrement" and left the inhospitable
Maracaibo region on the margins of the colony.*
—JAMES FERGUSON, VENEZUELA (1994)

IMPORTANCE OF OIL PRODUCTION

Technology has changed since the *conquistadors* dubbed oil
"the devil's excrement." If the Spaniards could travel in a
time machine to the present, they would be flabbergasted
to learn that this foul-smelling, gooey fluid is the modern world's
main source of fuel energy. They would be equally amazed to know

A man cycles past the Mene oil refinery run by the state oil firm Petróleos de Venezuela, in Maracaibo. Oil production is a major element of the financial success of Venezuela.

that the production of oil dominates Venezuela's modern economy. In fact, mining and refining oil accounts for almost 28 percent of the country's gross domestic product (GDP). The GDP is the value of all goods and services produced in a country in a given year.

The government-run *Petróleos de Venezuela* (Venezuelan Petroleum) controls the oil industry. Petroleum, which includes natural gas as well as oil, brings in about 50 percent of the government's revenue. Venezuelan Petroleum has lucrative contracts with foreign oil companies that drill for the country's petroleum. The most notable companies are American, like ConocoPhilips, Chevron, and Exxon-Mobil. Venezuelan Petroleum refines about one-third of the crude oil and all the natural gas that these ventures produce. The remaining crude oil is shipped to other countries (mainly the United States) for refining. Altogether, the country's crude and refined petroleum accounts for 80 percent of export earnings.

"SAUDI VENEZUELA" AND "SOWING THE OIL"

The first company to drill for oil in Venezuela was the Royal Dutch Shell Company (a business co-owned by investors from Great Britain and the Netherlands). Royal Dutch Shell first discovered oil in the Maracaibo Basin in 1917. In 1922, the company was drilling on the northeastern shore of Lake Maracaibo when suddenly it struck the Bolívar field, the largest deposit of oil outside the Middle East. The field is the third largest in the world.

After the discovery of the Bolívar field, Venezuela quickly became the world's leading oil exporter. Venezuela enjoyed an oil boom from 1950 to 1980, when huge amounts of money from oil exports poured into the country. Historians refer to Venezuela during its oil boom as "Saudi Venezuela," after Saudi Arabia, the world's leading oil producer at the dawn of the twenty-first century. Besides Saudi Arabia, several other countries are now producing more oil than Venezuela. The boom peaked about 1970, when oil made Venezuela South America's richest country and the world's leading oil producer. The country's share of the world's oil exports slowly decreased after the boom as large oil fields were discovered in other countries. Venezuela, however, still ranks among the top 10 countries in oil exports and oil reserves.

Arturo Uslar Pietri, the Venezuelan writer and politician, popularized the phrase "sowing the oil" to describe his country's policy of investing petrodollars in Venezuelan industries and businesses. Most of the money went to Venezuelan construction firms. The investments had a positive effect on the rest of the economy. Construction companies greatly expanded the physical infrastructure of streets, highways, bridges, communication systems, sewers, dams, and electric power lines. Venezuelan workers, in turn, spent their wages in businesses of a growing urban middle class. At the start of the twenty-first century, the government shifted more oil money to social programs, such as educational, housing and health services, than on infrastructure projects. The shift to social spending was a response to the growing political influence of barrio workers, who were dissatisfied over low wages, few jobs, and poor living conditions.

A TRADING NATION

Venezuela's main trading partner is by far the United States. Oil accounts for about 80 percent of the country's exports. U.S. markets take in much of the oil and account for about 50 percent of all exports. U.S. businesses supply about 30 percent of the Venezuela's imports. Venezuela's imports are lower in value than its exports, resulting in a trade surplus, or positive trade balance. The country is seeking to improve its trade surplus through Free Trade Agreements (FTAs). FTAs stimulate trade by reducing or eliminating tariffs (taxes on imports and exports) between trading partners. Venezuela has FTAs with the Caribbean Community and Common Market

(CARICOM), Colombia, and Mexico. Venezuela is an associate member of Mercosur (Argentina, Brazil, Paraguay and Uruguay). Membership in Mercosur allows Venezuela special trading access to South American neighbors.

Venezuela is also an original member of the World Trade Organization (WTO). The WTO operates a system of trade rules that all member nations are expected to follow. It is a place for them to discuss trade agreements and settle disputes between member countries. Venezuela is a founding member of the Organization of Petroleum Exporting Countries (OPEC), which has 11 member nations. Venezuela is the only OPEC member in Latin America. OPEC members coordinate their oil production policies to help stabilize the oil market and to help oil producers achieve a reasonable rate of return on their investments. This policy is supposed to ensure that oil consumers continue to receive stable supplies of oil, but oil prices still vary from month to month.

ECONOMIC REGIONS

Even though Venezuela's oil boom ended in 1980, oil continues to give Venezuela a trade surplus. All the same, the country is too dependent on this sole commodity. As the price of oil goes up or down, so does the nation's economy. A more diverse range of products would make the economy more stable. The government hopes to strengthen the country's various regional products in order to diversify the economy. The following paragraphs sum up each region's contribution to the nation's economy.

Northern Highlands

This region includes the nation's core area of population and economic activity. From colonial times, industry has focused on Caracas. During recent decades, however, the government started to disperse industry from the capital by spending oil money to build a highway system. The system started with a superhighway between Caracas and its seaport, La Guaira, in 1953. Bridges and tunnels replaced the old road's tortuous switchbacks and hairpin turns. The new route allowed the shipment of products from the Caracas Valley to docks in La Guaira in less than a half-hour. A demand for exports through La Guaira picked up dramatically once the superhighway opened. Jobs suddenly became available in Caracas as factories tried to keep up with growing demand. The city rapidly became overcrowded with poor people emigrating from the countryside to work in the factories.

The government responded by improving roads from the capital to other cities. The better roads promoted factory growth in other parts of the country. Valencia, Maracay, and several smaller cities near Caracas became part of the nation's economic heartland as a result. Today, this core area produces a variety of factory goods: textiles; foods and beverages; paper, stone and clay products; chemicals; and metalwork. Negative results from industrialization, however, have arisen. Poverty in rural areas pushed people to the cities in search of jobs and caused the overcrowded barrios. Industrial growth also led to serious problems of traffic congestion and pollution of air and water.

Agriculture is less important than industry and commerce in the highlands. Urban growth has pushed farmers out of larger valley floors, which have deep rich soils, and onto slopes that have shallow, less fertile soils. Farmers manage to make a meager income by selling vegetables (potatoes, garlic, onions, and carrots) and fruits (mangoes, oranges, and avocados) in small village markets. Hardly any of the locally grown produce is sold in large cities. Venezuela imports most of its food instead.

Coffee is the countryside's main export cash crop. Coffee plants take up more land than any other crop except corn, which is a food staple for the local people. Coffee thrives on sloping land, so the crop grows especially well in the Venezuelan Andes. The country, though, produces less than one percent of

Farmers work the fields in western Venezuela. Agriculture has taken a back seat to industry in certain parts of the nation. However, some farmers still manage to make meager profits from their crops.

the world's coffee crop. There are a few large, wealthy haciendas (cattle-raising estates) scattered in the mountains, but most haciendas are in the Llanos region.

Many of the Northern Highlands' rural folk are expert leather, textile, and wood artisans. To add to their income from crops, they sell leather goods (saddles, belts, hats, vests, packs) and rugs, ponchos, blankets, and woodcarvings in open-air markets. Local people buy the high-quality handicrafts for practical uses. Tourists sometimes visit the markets to buy the goods as souvenirs at bargain prices.

The Coast

Recreation and tourism thrive along most of Venezuela's coastline. The coast is a young economic region, so the road system is underdeveloped. Beaches are where stressed-out residents of Venezuela's highland cities most like to flock.

These urbanites just come for weekend visits. Other, wealthier Venezuelans have retirement or second homes there. These people were flush with money from the 1950–1980 oil boom and invested some of their wealth in coastal real estate. As a result, many small seaside resorts date from the boom period.

The verdant chain of mountains rising out of the sea is a perfect backdrop for this recreational getaway. The coast has three areas that cater to vacationers: the central, western, and eastern areas. Venezuelan vacationers are drawn to all three areas primarily for their stunning, palm-lined beaches. A modest number of foreign tourists are also drawn to the coast. They come from North America and Europe. A main attraction for them in the central area is sport fishing and skin diving at Los Roques (The Rocks), the country's main offshore archipelago. In the western area, foreign tourist attractions include island beaches, colossal sand dunes, and the colonial towns of Puerto Cabello and Coro. The eastern section of the coast draws foreign visitors to two additional colonial cities: Cumaná, which is South America's oldest city, and Barcelona. Near Barcelona is a large resort with first-class tourist hotels. Despite the fame of Cumaná and Barcelona, Margarita Island is the most popular eastern tourist resort. Another eastern lure is a scenic coastal high-way—"Route of the Sun"—that follows the Paria Peninsula's mountainous spine. The Orinoco Delta, which makes up the rest of the country's coastal region, faces the Atlantic Ocean. Tourists seldom visit the delta, as it has few towns and amenities for visitors.

Maracaibo Lowland

People avoided the Maracaibo Basin until the discovery of the Bolívar oil field in 1922. Oil production in the basin peaked in the mid-1970s. The Maracaibo oil fields once produced three-fourths of the country's petroleum. Today, slightly less than half the total production comes from there. (More oil

A young girl poles a boat to move between houses on stilts in a fishing village on Lake Maracaibo. The city of Maracaibo, like Caracas, also has a contrast between the wealthy lifestyle in the city to the poor in the rural areas.

comes from the Llanos region now.) The city of Maracaibo is a modern, expensive high-rise metropolis. The city is home to a cosmopolitan population of oil engineers and executives. Oil drilling, oil refining, and petrochemical (oil-related) industries are the Maracaibo Basin's main economic activities.

The rural landscape around Lake Maracaibo includes various forms of agriculture. A few commercial dairies are west of the lake. Wealthy landowners own large plantations of sugar cane, cacao, and coconuts along the lake's southern margins. Lakeside villages rely on fish, rice, and coconuts. On poorer land, the main livelihood is subsistence farming. Goats, cattle, pigs, hens, and a donkey or two are typical of every farm; so are small fields of corn, beans, and squash. In the tropical southern part of the lowland, farmers also grow plantains, papayas, and cassava in small forest clearings.

Orinoco Plains (Llanos)

Cattle, irrigated fields, and oil stamp a unity on the Llanos. The cattle industry dominates the region's wide-open spaces. The soil and a wet-dry tropical climate support the growth of grasses for the grazing animals. Local caudillos and late-arriving foreign land companies had divided the Llanos into large haciendas by the end of nineteenth century. Hacienda owners ignored cattle breeding, grazed the animals on poor pasture grasses, and allowed the skinny herds to roam freely over unfenced land. Landowners became wealthy from the cattle business, despite their poor methods of raising the animals, as a rising middle class in Europe and North America created a huge market for beef.

The government helped jumpstart small farms and encouraged better ranching methods in the Llanos after World War II. A government land reform program took over vast tracts of land in the northern Llanos not used by large haciendas. Officials then encouraged poor farmers in the highlands to resettle on the new land. The government built dams on rivers in the highlands to control flooding in the plains. Canals and pipelines from the dams also diverted water to the Llanos to irrigate pasture grasses and cash crops. (The region's dry summer requires the irrigation of pasture and crop land.) The first dam and large resettlement project was completed in the Llanos near Calabozo in 1956. Irrigation and resettlement projects have continued to expand, but at a slow pace. In the early 2000s, the Chávez government opened up more land west of Calabozo, in the states of Cojedes and Portuguesa.

Without the resettlement projects, population pressure in the Northern Highlands would be even greater than it is. Thousands of poor barrio dwellers have moved from there to the Llanos. They have built fences around their new land. Fencing helps to breed better strains of cattle and to grow better quality pasture grasses. Fencing also enables farmers to plant cash crops that free-roaming animals would otherwise eat. The plains region now has fields of maize, rice, sesame, sugar cane, cotton, and sorghum in places where there are fences and water for irrigation. Venezuela's cities are ready markets for the cash crops and animal products resulting from the resettlement projects. Still, flood control and irrigation have affected only a small fraction of the Llanos region.

Most of the region's agriculture depends on the large haciendas that focus on producing fresh beef for the urban markets of the Northern Highlands. Venezuelans today prefer to call cattle ranches *hatos*, rather than haciendas. Some hatos rely on ecotourism for extra income. They have built lodges for tourists and run tours to show guests the local wildlife. The ecotourism industry is so successful that some hatos are taking steps to protect their wildlife. They are setting up ecological research stations and contributing money to local environmental causes.

Venezuela's oil fields include a vast Orinoco Plains belt. Porous sedimentary rocks that lie beneath the northern half of the Llanos store the oil. This natural resource brings in more money to the Llanos region than any other economic activity. Drilling began in the 1930s, but on a small scale. The Orinoco oil belt produced about one-fourth of the nation's total crude oil by 1975. Now the area produces slightly more than half the total production, although Maracaibo oil is of better quality. The largest Orinoco oil fields are in the northeastern Llanos around the cities of Maturín and El Tigre. Another large field is near Barinas, which is in northwestern Llanos. The presence of oil led to important petrochemical industries in all three cities. Smaller fields lie in north-central Llanos. Oil pipelines connect the Orinoco fields to local refineries and to export facilities at Caribbean seaports.

Guiana Highlands

Mining, iron, steel, and electrical power generation dominate the economy of this region. In the vastness of the Guiana Highlands lie huge deposits of iron ore and bauxite (the raw material for aluminum). The region also has deposits of gold, silver, uranium, nickel, and phosphates.

Iron ore is the most abundant mineral of the region. After World War II, the great iron-ore deposits on the northern rim of the plateau attracted the former giants of the U.S. steel industry—the U.S. Steel and Bethlehem Steel corporations—to the region. Both companies had large open-pit mines. The main U.S. Steel mine was the entire top of the mountain Cerro Bolívar. Bethlehem Steel's main mine was nearby at the town of El Piar. These companies mined the ore and shipped it by rail to barges on the Orinoco River. The barges took the ore to the Paria Peninsula. There it was loaded on ocean-going ore carriers for export to the United States.

The Venezuelan government took over the iron-mining operations and related facilities in 1975. Since then, rather than exporting the iron ore as the U.S. companies did, the government processes it into iron and steel at its plants at Ciudad Guayana. This city was born in 1961, when government planners fused two other cities, Puerto Ordaz and San Félix. Ciudad Guayana is where the Caroní River flows into the Orinoco River. The confluence of the rivers makes it easier to transport iron ore and various minerals from the highlands to processing plants in Ciudad Guayana. River barges use the Orinoco to transport processed steel, iron ore, aluminum, and minerals (like gold) from the city to ocean-going vessels downriver. The largest market for Venezuelan steel is the domestic oil industry. Venezuelan Petroleum needs structural steel and iron, and steel pipes. Some iron and steel products are exported.

Because of the iron and steel industry, Ciudad Guayana is one of Venezuela's fastest-growing urban centers. The city's population is expected to reach 2 million by 2030.

Development of hydroelectric power made the city's industrial growth possible. Water power generates electricity in dams built on rivers flowing from the Guiana Highlands, especially the Caroní. Guiana's hydroelectric power plants also provide most of the rest of the country's energy needs. Transmission lines feed the electricity to Caracas and other large cities. The country also sells electricity from the Guiana Highlands to Colombia and Brazil.

GROWING ECONOMIC WOES OF THE NEW CENTURY

As we have seen, Venezuela's economic regions provide a diversity of incomes. Petrodollars, however, are by far the main contributor to economic growth. The annual supply of investment money grew during the 1950–1980 oil boom, but the actual contributions to the economy grew in increasingly lesser amounts. Five main reasons led to the decline in investment. First, the growth of oil earnings slowed down, as the rivalry with other oil-producing countries for markets slowed the growth of oil exports. Second, the government was borrowing huge sums of money (that it could not pay back) to finance ambitious health, education, and transportation projects. The government had to use petrodollars to pay interest on the loans. Third, government policies discouraged the investing of money to produce consumer goods. It encouraged investing instead in the petroleum and petrochemical industry. As a result, Venezuelans had to send money to other countries to pay for imported food and other basic consumer items.

The supply of investment money also shrank because of corrupt Venezuelan officials. These officials stole (embezzled) large sums of petrodollars. They hid some of the money in foreign bank accounts. They spent the rest on luxury items produced in foreign factories, such as yachts, BMWs, jewelry, and fur coats. A fifth reason that the supply of petrodollars shrank is that newly rich middle-class Venezuelans went on spending sprees in foreign countries. Miami, Florida, became the favorite shopping spot. "It's cheap, I'll take two" was the motto of a typical Venezuelan shopper in Miami during the economic boom. For all these reasons, Venezuela lost money that could have been invested in Venezuelan businesses. Businesses, in turn, created fewer jobs, so that there was less money in the form of wages to increase the demand for Venezuelan goods and services.

By 2000, the post-boom downturn was dramatic. Industries had to lay off workers, as businesses had little money to purchase raw materials. Nearly one in five Venezuelans was unemployed. About half the population was living in poverty. Consumer prices were chronically high and rising. The cash-starved economy raised political unrest between the rich and poor to a fever pitch. Workers poured into the streets to protest against the government. To make matters worse, amid the political instability, foreign businesses not involved in the oil economy began pulling money out of the country.

CHAPTER

7

Living in Venezuela Today

Nearly 90 percent of Venezuelans are urbanites (city dwellers). Life in larger cities, like Caracas or Maracaibo, appears to have the harried pace of any big city in the world. Venezuelans, though, know how to take it easy. For instance, urbanites have kept the countryside's custom of the *siesta*—a long rest period after a mid-day lunch. Thus, they are accustomed to starting work early at 7 or 8 A.M., but finishing late at 6 or 7 P.M.

FOOD AND MEALS

A typical day for Venezuelans includes three meals: breakfast, lunch, and dinner. They refer collectively to their dishes as *comida criolla* (Creole food). Creole food includes plenty of meat, rice, yams, plantains, beans, and seafood. The nation's distinctive cultural regions add a mix of local products to meals. Among other things, the Caribbean Sea provides a wide range of seafood; the coastal plain yields sweet coconut milk and chocolate; the mountains supply coffee, wheat, potatoes and trout; the Llanos region yields juicy beef; and Amazonas produces cassava (yucca) and exotic dishes like deep-fried ants.

Most Venezuelan meals include mouth-watering *arepas* and *empanadas*. Arepas are puffy, fist-size biscuits of fried or baked corn flour dough (corn meal). Empanadas are corn turnovers. They are smaller versions of arepas. Inside arepas and empanadas are fillings of virtually anything imaginable: Chicken salad, shredded beef, tuna salad, deviled ham, or grated cheeses are common. Some stuffing even has bits of octopus and baby shark. Venezuelans call their restaurants *areperas*, as arepas are common in Venezuelan meals.

Breakfast (*desayuno*) is a light meal. Often people grab a fresh arepa at a bakery shop (*panadería*) on their way to work. Lunch (*almuerzo*) is the main meal. Customarily, this meal is a drawn-out social affair: It lasts about two hours, followed by a one-hour siesta. Lunch is usually high in calories. The most common dish, and some would say the national dish, is *pabellón*. It includes deep-fried plantains, thin strips of beef, grated cheese, and a fried egg piled on top of black beans and rice. Increasingly, downtown businesses of the largest cities are shortening the lunch break because of the pressures of competition and long commute times to and from work. Office workers and managers must substitute sandwiches at fast-food restaurants for a big lunch, so that they can go back to work after only an hour or two. One or more arepas suffice for dinner (*comida*), if lunch was filling enough. Otherwise, dinner is a cooked meal, similar to lunch but smaller.

Spanish, Italian, Chinese, Thai, and Middle Eastern restaurants contribute a cosmopolitan flair to the nation's palate. In Caracas, especially, foreign-owned fast-food restaurant chains—Subway, McDonald's, Kentucky Fried Chicken (KFC) and Burger King—appeal to the harried lifestyle of a big city.

A Venezuelan food staple, *arepas* can be filled with just about anything one can imagine. Here, workers eat and sell *arepas*, which some poor families eat as their basic meal.

Not to be outdone, Venezuelan street vendors provide their own spicy versions of the American hamburger and hot dog. A choice of *salsas* (sauces) accompanies these sandwiches, as they do all meals. Sweet peppers and coriander (cilantro) leaves are main salsa flavorings. Popular alternatives are Worcestershire sauce and *salsa rosada* (pink sauce), a blend of ketchup and mayonnaise.

DRESSING UP

Styles of dress vary greatly in Venezuela. For the most remote Indian tribes, who live in the humid tropical areas of the Amazonas Plain and the Orinoco Delta, it is perfectly all right for women to be topless and both men and women to wear only a loincloth. Frequent cloud cover and the shade of the tropical rain forest reduce the danger of too much sun on the skin. Everywhere else, the wearing of clothes is a basic social rule. But people of various regions and cultures prefer certain articles of clothing. In some cases, choices are influenced by environmental conditions. For instance, in the cool Andes, almost everyone wears a woolen poncho. Likewise, the llanero cowboy dons a broad-brimmed, coarsely woven straw hat for protection from the sun. During "winter" evenings, however, a poncho might drape his shoulders.

City people abandon ponchos and straw hats for modern-style clothing. In hot climates of the valleys and plains, cotton is the fabric of choice, because it better protects the wearer from the stifling tropical heat. Appearing up to date, though, is more important than being comfortable. Thus, whenever an item of warm clothing becomes fashionable, tropical temperatures become less important than style. In this regard, any hint of body odor brought on by perspiration is a social blunder for either sex. Venezuelans shower at least twice daily and always change clothes after work.

Generally, urban men prefer white or neutral pastel-colored clothing. Women favor brighter colors. Professional women wear modern pantsuits while they are at work. Professional men reject the European-American jacket and tie as formal attire. They prefer the *liqui-liqui*, a button-down jacket with a high collar and matching pants. Both sexes prefer wearing shorts, T-shirts, and sandals when they are at home with close family members and friends.

Venezuelan women feel extraordinary pressure from society to be glamorous. Indeed, Venezuelan contestants won or were among the top-five finalists in the Miss Universe pageant every year from 1983 to 2003. A steady stream of beauty queens reflects Venezuelan society's fixation on feminine appearance. Feminine glamour means fussing over hair and makeup, and wearing skin-tight dresses with plenty of cleavage. Part of being glamorous also means wearing an entirely new outfit to every social event, or at least a prominent item of new clothing. Even in rural areas, where customary ways of living are stronger than in the cities, women feel they must dress up in trendy clothes. Traditional women's attire of the countryside consists of loose-fitting blouses and wide skirts with colorful patterns. This apparel is usually stored in closets, to be worn on appropriate social occasions, like folk festivals.

Social pressure to dress up is much less strong toward men than women. In *Culture Shock! Venezuela*, Kitt Baguley wrote that in public parks "you will see women who have obviously spent hours getting ready arm in arm with guys in jeans and a T-shirt." If they have to, however, Venezuelan men look sharp at social events. They wear tailored jackets, pressed trousers, and a narrow-rimmed, finely woven hat that resembles a Panama hat on important occasions. They sometimes wear the hat on informal occasions as well, although an American baseball cap is a popular substitute.

AMERICAN INFLUENCES

American culture adds a colorful layer of material culture to the everyday lives of Venezuelans. Material culture involves a taste for certain kinds of clothes, hairstyles, music, sports, and food. TV programming, Internet ads, movies, and billboards all push American material culture. What is more, American fast-food restaurants are not hard to find in the country's larger cities. Such eateries influence culture by changing traditional foods eaten by Venezuelan families. These influences are largely superficial. That is, they do not pass on great, problem-solving ideas, they simply persuade Venezuelans to buy American-made items. Venezuelan businesses market similar products because American goods are so popular.

American cultural influence has surpassed that of Europe. American baseball versus European football (soccer) is an example of the lopsided nature of American influence. Soccer reigns in every South American country except Venezuela. Venezuelans play and watch soccer and baseball, but baseball is king.

Venezuelans began playing baseball in Caracas in 1895. In 1941, Venezuela caught the eye of American baseball scouts when the national team won the fourth World Series of Amateur Baseball. Hoping to attract good baseball players, American Major League teams started a professional winter league in Venezuela in 1945. The first Venezuelan to play regularly in the United States was Alfonso "Chico" Carrasequel, who became the starting shortstop for the Chicago White Sox in 1950. Other great Venezuelan players who made it to the big leagues include Hall-of-Famer Luís Aparicio, David Concepción, Antonio Armas, Andrés *El Gran Gato* ("the big cat") Galarraga, Omar Vizquel, and Bobby Abreu. These and other Venezuelan baseball players have been idols and sources of inspiration for young men. Venezuela ranks second among foreign countries with players on Major League baseball teams.

ROLE OF WOMEN IN SOCIETY

When a young, single Hispanic woman walks down a street, men will often whistle and call to her to show approval of her appearance. Such behavior is a Hispanic man's way of expressing his manliness, or *machismo.* Stereotypically macho men also oppose a woman's right to work, participate in sports, or pursue other traditionally male roles in society. Venezuelan men share the trait of *machismo* with men of other Latin American countries.

Venezuelan women do not fit the stereotype of stay-at-home Latin American females. Many hold prominent positions in private businesses, political parties, and labor unions. On two occasions, political parties have even nominated women for president. For example, Irene Sáez went from being Miss Universe, to being mayor of Chacao (a district of Caracas), to being a presidential candidate in 1998.

Venezuelan women are motivated to get an education. This fact is an important reason for their success in business and other professional careers. More women than men

Youngsters play a game of baseball along a busy highway in Bejuma, Venezuela. The nation has quickly become a source of Major League talent, and has supplied American baseball with many recent stars.

graduate from high school in Venezuela than in any other Latin American country. Moreover, almost as many women as men graduate from universities. (Typically, male graduates outnumber female graduates by relatively wide margins in Latin America.) In some fields of study, women actually outnumber men in graduating classes. Thus, it is common to meet women in Venezuela with university degrees who are lawyers, business executives, medical doctors, judges, engineers, and architects.

Despite the progress women have made in Venezuelan society, they still do not have equal status with men. For instance, few women are elected to state or national political offices. What is more, the average income of women is about 30 percent less than that of men. All the same, the social advancement of Venezuela's females outshines the progress of their Hispanic sisters in other Latin American countries.

EDUCATION

The progress of women is proof that Venezuela has one of the best educational systems in Latin America. The literacy rate—people over 15 years of age who can read and write—is 93 percent. Literacy is high in part because going to school is free and compulsory for children ages 6 to 15. After graduating from primary school, students ages 15 to 18 choose to attend a vocational school or a secondary school. Studies in vocational schools include technical training in the industrial, agricultural, commercial, administrative, and health sectors. The training prepares students for better-paying industrial jobs. Secondary school provides a solid general education in science, art, and humanities, but students can also graduate with a specialization, like chemistry, art history, or a foreign language. Secondary school graduates are eligible to continue their education at a college or university. People take this path when they want to be teachers, doctors, lawyers, and business executives.

Unfortunately, Venezuela's economy is so poor that having an education does not guarantee a job. As a result, many youths quit before graduating from high school. The dropout rate is highest in the poverty-stricken barrios. Venezuela has a serious crime problem in the barrios, in part because dropouts are involved in the illegal drug trade and other criminal activities.

ILLEGAL DRUG TRADE AND CRIME

Venezuela's illegal drug problem is much worse than that of most countries. Drugs are abundant and relatively cheap, as Colombia, Venezuela's western neighbor, is the world's main source of cocaine and South America's leading producer of heroin. Major drug-trading routes from Colombia pass through Venezuela on their way to North American and European markets. Venezuelan middlemen keep part of the narcotics. They sell them at low prices to the unemployed youths of the barrios. These youths are easy targets, because getting high on drugs offers them a brief escape from the misery of boredom and poverty. Some youths also see a chance to make money by becoming street-level drug pushers for the middlemen. Their customers range from friends in barrios to executives in the downtown business districts. A whirlwind of drug addiction and crime affects everyone involved. Middlemen, street pushers, and customers become addicts. The addicts commit petty theft to feed their drug habits. Their crimes spiral upward to carjacking, bank robbery, kidnapping, or prostitution as their addiction grows.

Most murders in Venezuela involve drugs. Life becomes terribly cheap, and people die over arguments concerning girlfriends and drug deals. In 2000, Venezuela had 0.34 murders for every 1,000 people in its population. It ranked second in the world behind Colombia, which had 0.62 murders per 1,000 people. Most killings occur in Caracas. About 2,000 murders were reported in the city in 2002. Caracas's homicide rate was three times the national rate that year. Many barrio youths eventually join criminal gangs for mutual protection.

HEALTH CARE

Medicine is a highly respected profession in Venezuela, but a shortage of doctors and adequately trained nurses exists. In particular, rural areas and barrios have less available health care than the wealthy areas of cities. *Barrio Adentro* ("Inside the neighborhood") is a cooperative program between Venezuela and Cuba to provide free health care to the underserved areas. The program began in 2003. Cuba's role in the program is to provide doctors and to train doctors

A Cuban doctor sees her patient, in an office in La Guaira, Venezuela. The doctor is one of several hundred brought in from Cuba by President Chávez in exchange for refined oil.

and nurses. At least 15,000 Cuban doctors have been put to work in Venezuela. Venezuela's role includes building medical clinics in poor areas and housing for the doctors. As part of the deal, the Venezuelan government pays the doctors much more than they would earn in Cuba and provides Cuba with oil at below-market rates.

Barrio Adentro has drawn praise from the Latin American branch of the World Health Organization. The program, however, is charged with political controversy because it was conceived through the friendship of Hugo Chávez, Venezuela's president, and Fidel Castro, Cuba's communist dictator. Chávez's political opponents charge that the Cuban *Barrio Adentro* doctors are communist agents who want to convert the Venezuelan population to communism. The Venezuelan Ministry of Health counters that the program is necessary to provide health care in poor areas. The ministry claims that millions of people have been treated through *Barrio Adentro.*

TRANSPORTATION

Venezuelans drive more cars per populated area than any other Latin American country, except Chile. People living in the suburbs own most of the cars, and they prefer to drive to work. They are a little crazy when it comes to driving. Drivers usually ignore laws for speed limits and seat belts. Cars are affordable partly because Venezuela produces its own gasoline, making the price of fuel relatively cheap. As a result, highways and streets are usually jammed with commuters during morning and afternoon rush hours.

Many Venezuelans cannot afford cars, despite the low price of fuel. Low-priced public transportation is readily available. The cheapest form of public transportation is the city bus (*transporte* or *colectivo*). The minibus, another form of public transportation, is a little more expensive, but it can meander through chaotic traffic faster than the regular city bus. Taxis (*libres*), which many Venezuelans cannot afford, circulate constantly in downtown areas looking for wealthy executives and tourists.

Caracas is the only city in Venezuela with a subway system, but it does not serve enough of the city to reduce traffic congestion. Riding bicycles would be an alternative, but the country is not friendly to bicyclists. Roads do not have bicycle lanes, and motorists do not give bicyclists any rights of way.

Most Venezuelans travel between cities by bus, as buses are generally fast, run regularly day and night, and are reasonably priced. Airlines that fly modern passenger jets serve most large cities. A first-rate network of light planes travels secondary air routes to smaller cities. Passenger airliners also connect Caracas and Maracaibo to neighboring capitals and to cities in North America and Europe. The safety record of Venezuelan air travel is very good. Still, airline tickets are too expensive for most Venezuelans. There is no intercity passenger train service in Venezuela, as the government chose to stop paying for the upkeep of railroads decades ago.

Commercial freight hauling relies mainly on 18-wheel trucks. These monster trucks carry maritime ship cargo containers to and from Venezuela's busy seaports. Out-of-the-way places in the Llanos, Guiana Highlands, and Amazonas regions depend more on small cargo planes than do other parts of the country. The only railroad freight line in operation runs between Valencia and its seaport, Puerto Cabello.

There is hardly any overland freight traffic between Venezuela and its neighbors, as few transport routes cross its borders. There is no cross-border railroad connection any-where. Moreover, there is no car or truck link with Guyana; a traveler must go there in a roundabout way via Brazil. The only road connecting Venezuela to Brazil is a mostly gravel surface linking Manaus, which is in the heart of Brazil's Amazon rain forest, to Ciudad Guayana. Only four roads for cars and trucks cross between Venezuela and Colombia. The main crossing is in the Andes between Táchira, Venezuela, and Cúcuta, Colombia.

MEDIA AND ELECTRONIC COMMUNICATIONS

The constitution provides for freedom of speech and the press. The government, however, has the power to give and take away licenses to Venezuelan journalists and broadcast stations if they are too critical of how the country is run. What is more, the president has the power to have Venezuelan journalists arrested if they cast the government in an unfavor-able light. The media are also under pressure to say good things about the government, because the government pays the media large sums of money for public sector advertising. Despite these outside pressures, Venezuela's newspapers and broadcast (radio and TV) media claim to represent facts without favoring one political point of view or another.

Even with serious turmoil surrounding real-world national politics, fantasy soap operas (*telenovelas*) are the most watched programs on television. They are like American soap operas; the actors are remarkably good-looking, and the characters all seem to lead dramatic and complex lives. Venezuelan production companies make the telenovelas and distribute them throughout Latin America. The Venezuelan telenovela business is a multimillion-dollar industry. In 2005, the Chávez government announced the creation of Telesur, a proposed Latin America-wide satellite television network to compete with the Spanish edition of CNN and Univision, the largest Spanish-speaking TV outlets in the Western Hemisphere.

The two leading Caracas newspapers, *El Universal* and *El Nacional,* have countrywide distribution. They cover national and international affairs, sports, economics, and culture. The *Daily Journal* is the main English-language newspaper. Venezuela has five commercial TV channels. The usual mix of news, sports, films, and entertainment is available on cable as well. The programming reflects the nation's penchant for glamour, as impossibly beautiful women (usually with blonde hair) host game and talk shows, forecast weather, and report the news. Venezuelan radio is largely regional in focus, as most radio stations cover a state or just one city. The stations offer a variety of programs along with commercial breaks for local businesses.

The Internet industry is small. About 50 of every 1,000 Venezuelans go online, whereas nearly 600 of every 1,000 Americans do. Few Venezuelans have personal computers. Consequently, Internet cafés are popular. These are small stores where, for a small fee, people can send and receive e-mail messages and browse the Web. Cellphones in Venezuela are rapidly replacing landline telephones, but Venezuelan cellphone users are still outnumbered by U.S. users three to one.

WEIGHTS AND MEASURES, TIME, AND HOLIDAYS

Venezuela uses the metric system rather than English system of weights and measures. Grams and kilograms appear on packages, not ounces and pounds. Meters and kilometers designate distances, not feet and miles. Hectares, not acres, refer to areas.

The country is four hours behind Greenwich Mean Time (or universal time coordinates). If it is 3 P.M. in Caracas, it will be 7 P.M. in Greenwich, England. (The Eastern time zone of the United States is five hours behind Greenwich Mean Time.) Venezuela does not observe daylight savings time. In other words, Venezuelans do not turn their clocks ahead an hour in the spring ("spring forward") and back an hour in the fall ("fall back") to have an extra hour of daylight during the summer.

The country has several public holidays when most shops, offices, and museums are closed. Venezuelans celebrate Christmas on December 25 and New Year's Day with fireworks on January 1. Two holidays that fall close to each other are Carnival and Easter. They reflect the two sides of Venezuelans. Carnival is carefree and celebratory, while Easter is subdued and reverent. Carnival officially takes place in February or early March on the Monday and Tuesday before Lent. Unofficially, celebrating lasts for days. City-dwellers like to travel to pleasure spots along the Caribbean coast during this holiday. Lively music, sensual dancing, devil masks, and colorful costumes flood the streets of most cities.

Easter's quiet penance replaces the festive mood of Carnival. Easter occurs in March or April. People stay at home or visit relatives who live nearby on this occasion. Thursday and Friday of Easter week are official holidays. Families observe Easter

Sunday by attending or participating in religious processions and Catholic Masses. Additional holidays include: Declaration of Independence (April 19); International Workers' Day (May 1); Anniversary of the Battle of Carabobo, the turning point in the War of Independence (June 24); Independence Day (July 5); birth of Simón Bolívar (July 24); and Columbus Day (October 12).

8

Venezuela Looks Ahead

V enezuela has struggled ever since Columbus claimed the territory for Spain. The Spanish Crown neglected the new colony almost from the beginning. There was no silver and very little gold to hold the Crown's interest in the colony. Spanish *conquistadors* quickly depleted the region's supplies of pearls and Indian slaves. Spain gave little protection to Venezuela's seaports. Spanish warships were sent off to guard gold- and silver-laden *flotas* plying Caribbean waters farther north. Pirates were free to troll the colony's shores and to plunder the poorly protected coastal towns.

Independence was not kind to Venezuela either. Weak post-colonial governments prevented the young country from developing its potential as a nation. While other countries progressed, Venezuela became a poor backwater. It was not until the mid- twentieth century that petrodollars from the sale of oil transformed the economy. Venezuela became one of the world's wealthiest countries during the

The youth of Venezuela face many challenges in the years to come. With a sagging economy and an outbreak of corruption and crime, the nation looks to its young to help pave the way to a brighter future.

1950s and 1960s. During this heyday, the government invested petrodollars in the national infrastructure, including roads, schools, water supply, electric grid, and so on. Venezuelans were brimming with self-confidence. In 1950, the per-capita GDP ranked fourth-highest in the world. The economy nosedived around 1980, however, and Venezuela's current struggles began. By 2003, the nation's revenues had plummeted from 4th to 110th among the world's 190 nations.

Venezuela faces many challenges today. The roots of its economic tree are clearly in need of more and better monetary nourishment. The days of free spending are gone. Billions of borrowed dollars must be paid back to foreign banks. Foreign businesses, which bring badly needed investment money, are pulling out of the country because of ongoing problems of corruption, crime, and social unrest. The government hopes to improve its economy by cleaning up corruption and crime and bringing back foreign investment. Additionally, as a trading nation, Venezuela relies too heavily on a single export— petroleum. It hopes to develop the economies of its various regions to diversify exports.

Social and environmental problems exist as well. Economic growth brought on by oil production has masked fermenting social unrest among the nation's poor. The government is funneling more oil money to social programs and resettlement projects to help bridge the divide between the haves and have-nots. However, poverty-ridden *barrios* desperately need many more jobs, schools, and health clinics. Moreover, throughout cities in general, drug addiction, crime, congested freeways, longer commuting times, and pollution are having a negative effect on living conditions. Additionally, demands on soil, forest, and ocean resources are increasing. As a result, fertile land for agriculture, habitat for wildlife species, and tropical rain forests are disappearing.

A political divide between the haves and have-nots also threatens Venezuela. For many years, the country enjoyed limited democratic rule by two parties. The two-party system ignored the growing poverty among rural and city workers. Workers had no political party to represent them. Isolation of the poor ended in the late 1990s with the emergence of Hugo Chávez, who has completely changed Venezuela's political life. He was elected president because of the grassroots support of millions of poor people, those who the traditional political parties ignored. Through democratic elections, Chávez's party—Movement of the Fifth Republic (MVR)—gained control of the legislature. The legislature, in turn, gave him powers similar to those of a dictator.

Rather than trying to heal divisions between the social classes, Chávez is dividing the country even further. He blames the wealthier middle and upper classes and the traditional political parties for the nation's poverty. His faithful supporters, who come from the barrios and poor countryside, liken him to Simón Bolívar, hero of the nineteenth-century independence wars. He is expanding resettlement projects in the countryside. He is also bringing in Cuban doctors to barrios and rural areas. Chávez's detractors accuse him of being too close to Fidel Castro, Cuba's communist dictator. They fear that he is dragging the country down the Cuban path of communism.

Venezuela's future is worrisome to the United States and the world. The Latin American country is the largest exporter of oil in the Western Hemisphere, and much of this valuable resource goes to the United States. Yet, at the dawn of the twenty-first century, the nation is at a troublesome crossroad in its evolution. The crossroad has three paths: democracy, dictatorship, or communism. Democracy has given Venezuela some economic stability, but as we have seen, it still has many problems. On the other hand, the path to dictatorship or to communism could lead to political violence and greater instability. Only the future will tell what direction Venezuela will take.

Facts at a Glance

Physical Geography

Total Area	352,143 square miles (912,050 square kilometers)
Climate	Tropical; hot, humid; more moderate temperatures in the highlands
Terrain	Andes Mountains and Maracaibo Basin in the northwest; coastal hills in the north-central and northeast; central plains (Llanos); Guiana Highlands in the southeast
Highest Point	Pico Bolívar 16,427 feet (5,007 meters)
Natural Resources	Petroleum, natural gas, iron ore, gold, bauxite, other minerals, hydropower, diamonds
Land Use	Arable land (2.95 percent); permanent crops (0.92 percent); other (96.13 percent)
Irrigated Land	208.5 square miles (540 square kilometers)
Natural Hazards	Floods, landslides, mudslides; periodic droughts

People

Population	25,375,281 (July 2005 estimate)
Population Growth Rate	1.4 percent (2005 estimate)
Net Migration Rate	0 migrant(s)/1,000 population (2005 estimate)
Life Expectancy at Birth	74 years (2004 estimate)
Ethnic Groups	Spanish, Italian, Portuguese, Arab, German, African, indigenous people
Religions	Roman Catholic 96 percent, Protestant 2 percent, other 2 percent
Language	Spanish (official), numerous indigenous dialects
Literacy	93.4 percent (age 15 and over who can read and write)

Government

Government Type	Federal Republic
Capital	Caracas
Administrative Divisions	23 states, 1 federal district, 1 federal dependency**; Amazonas, Anzoátegui, Apure, Aragua, Barinas, Bolívar, Carabobo, Cojedes, Delta Amarcuro, Dependencias Federales**, Districto Federal, Falcón, Guárico, Lara, Mérida, Miranda, Monagas, Nueva Esparta, Portuguesa, Sucre, Táchira, Trujillo, Vargas, Yaracuy, Zulia
Note:	The federal dependency consists of 11 federally controlled island groups with a total of 72 islands.

Economy

GDP $145.2 billion (2004 estimate)

Labor Force by Occupation   Agriculture 13 percent; industry 23 percent; services 64 percent (1997 estimate)

Industries   Petroleum, iron ore mining, construction materials, food processing, textiles, steel, aluminum, motor vehicle assembly

Agricultural Products   Corn, sorghum, sugar cane, rice, bananas, vegetables, coffee, beef, pork, milk, eggs, fish

Export Commodities   Petroleum, bauxite and aluminum, steel, chemicals, agricultural products, basic manufactures

Exports–Main Partners   United States 58.7 percent, Netherlands Antilles 4.1 percent, Canada 2.5 percent (2004)

Import Commodities   Raw materials, machinery and equipment, transport equipment, construction materials

Imports–Main Partners   United States 33.2 percent, Colombia 5.7 percent, Brazil 5 percent, Germany 4 percent (2004)

History at a Glance

1498	Christopher Columbus visits Venezuela.
1499	Alonzo de Ojeda (or Hojeda) names Venezuela.
1520	Earliest Spanish settlements begin on the northeast coast.
1528–1546	Spain gives administrative control of the colony to German bankers.
1577	Caracas officially becomes capital of the colony.
1728–1789	Spain gives economic control of the colony to the Caracas Company.
1811	Independence Act is signed, and War of Independence is led by Simón Bolívar.
1812	Powerful earthquake strikes Caracas.
1830	Simón Bolívar dies of tuberculosis.
	Venezuela secedes from Gran Colombia and becomes an independent republic with its capital at Caracas. The reign of the caudillos begins.
1917	Royal Dutch Shell Company discovers oil in the Maracaibo Basin.
1930	A 40-year period of European immigration begins.
1935	The reign of the caudillos ends at a time when Venezuela is the world's largest exporter of oil.
1948	President Rómulo Gallegos, Venezuela's first democratically elected leader, is overthrown.
1950	The Venezuelan oil boom begins.
	Two U.S. corporations, Bethlehem Steel and U.S. Steel, begin mining operations in the Guiana Highlands.
1958	A military coup forces Venezuela's last dictator to flee the country.
	The *Punto Fijo* deal makes political parties legal.
	President Rómulo Betancourt is elected democratically in December, and the people have chosen Venezuela's presidents ever since.
1960	Venezuela and four other nations found OPEC (Organization of Petroleum Exporting Countries).
1961	Venezuela adopts a constitution that gives a wide variety of social rights to the people.
	Government begins creation of Ciudad Guayana.

1967 Communist Party, in effect, ends a Cuban-supported revolt by withdrawing from FALN (Armed Forces of National Liberation).

1973 Venezuela benefits from oil boom, and the value of its currency peaks against the U.S. dollar.

1975 Government takes over (nationalizes) the mining operations in the Guiana Highlands.

1980 The Venezuelan oil boom ends.

1983 Fall in world oil prices generates unrest and cuts in welfare spending.

1993 Venezuelan Supreme Court forces President Carlos Andrés Pérez to leave office by constitutional means.

1998 Hugo Chávez organizes the Movement of the Fifth Republic (MRV) and wins the presidential election.

1999 A new constitution expands presidential powers, extends presidential term from four to six years, and calls for new election in 2000.

2000 Chávez is elected to a six-year term as president.

2003 In cooperation with Cuba, Chávez's administration starts the *Barrio Adentro* health program.

2004 Chávez wins a recall referendum, so that he remains president until at least the next presidential election in 2006.

2005 Chávez administration opens up more land in the Llanos region for resettlement.

Bibliography

Antell, Claire, and Nick Caistor. *Insight Guide: Venezuela*. Maspeth, NY: Langenscheidt Publishers Inc., 2002.

Baguley, Kitt. *Culture Shock!: Venezuela*. Portland, OR: Graphic Arts Center Publishing Company, 1999.

Central Intelligence Agency. *CIA Fact Book*. Washington, D.C.: U.S. Government Printing Office, 2003.

Ferguson, James. *Venezuela: A Guide to the People, Politics and Culture*. London, England: Latin America Bureau, 1994.

Gallegos, Rómulo. *Doña Barbara*. New York: Johnathan Cape and Harrison Smith, 1931; Trans. by Robert Malloy, 1948.

Helferich, Gerard. *Humboldt's Cosmos: Alexander von Humboldt and the Latin American Journey That Changed the Way We See the World*. New York: Gotham Books, 2004.

Lombardi, John V. *Venezuela: The Search for Order, the Dream of Progress*. New York: Oxford University Press, 1982.

Uslar Pietri, Arturo. *The Red Lances*. New York: Knopf Publishing Company, 1931; Trans. by Harriet de Onis, 1963.

Index

Index

page:

9: © Lucidity Information Design
11: AFP/NMI
14: Zuma Press/NMI
16: © Lucidity Information Design
20: EPA Photos/NMI
25: New Millennium Images
28: New Millennium Images
34: Reuters/NMI
37: Zuma Press/NMI
45: EPA Photos/NMI
49: Zuma Press/NMI

53: EPA Photos/NMI
59: AFP/NMI
64: AFP/NMI
67: AFP/NMI
70: AFP/NMI
75: Reuters Photo Archive/NMI
77: Zuma Press/NMI
85: AP Photo/Natacha Pisarenko
89: KRT/NMI
92: Zuma Press/NMI
99: Reuters/NMI

Cover: Associated Press/AP

About the Contributors

DR. RICHARD A. CROOKER is a geography professor at Kutztown University in Pennsylvania, where he teaches physical geography, oceanography, map reading, and climatology. He received a Ph.D. in geography from the University of California, Riverside. Dr. Crooker is a member of the Association of American Geographers and the National Council for Geographic Education. He has received numerous research grants, including three from the National Geographic Society. His publications deal with a wide range of geographical topics. He enjoys reading, hiking, bicycling, and boogie boarding.

CHARLES F. "FRITZ" GRITZNER is Distinguished Professor of Geography at South Dakota University in Brookings. He is now in his fifth decade of college teaching and research. During his career, he has taught more than 60 different courses, spanning the fields of physical, cultural, and regional geography. In addition to his teaching, he enjoys writing, working with teachers, and sharing his love for geography with students. As consulting editor for the MODERN WORLD NATIONS series, he has a wonderful opportunity to combine each of these "hobbies." Fritz has served as both President and Executive Director of the National Council for Geographic Education and has received the Council's highest honor, the George J. Miller Award for Distinguished Service. In March 2004, he won the Distinguished Teaching award from the Association of American Geographers at their annual meeting held in Philadelphia.